INSIDE JURORS' MINDS: THE HIERARCHY OF JUROR DECISION-MAKING

THE TRIAL LAWYER'S GUIDE
TO UNDERSTANDING HOW JURORS THINK

INSIDE JURORS' MINDS: THE HIERARCHY OF JUROR DECISION-MAKING

A PRIMER ON THE PSYCHOLOGY OF PERSUASION:
THE TRIAL LAWYER'S GUIDE
TO UNDERSTANDING HOW JURORS THINK

Carol B. Anderson

Address inquiries to:
National Institute for Trial Advocacy
1685 38th Street, Suite 200
Boulder, CO 80301-2735
Phone: (800) 225-6482
Fax: (720) 890-7069
E-mail: permissions@nita.org

Library of Congress Cataloging-in-Publication Data
Anderson, Carol B. (Carol Boyles)
   Inside jurors' minds : the hierarchy of juror decision- making : a primer on the psychology of persuasion : a trial lawyer's guide to understanding how jurors think / by Carol B. Anderson.
      p. cm.
   ISBN 978-1-60156-181-7
   1. Jury--United States--Decision making. 2. Trial practice--United States--Psychological aspects. I. Title. II. Title: Hierarchy of juror decision- making. III. Title: Primer on the psychology of persuasion. IV. Title: Trial lawyer's guide to understanding how jurors think.
   KF8972.A855 2012
   347.73'752--dc23

                              2011053190

ISBN 978-1-60156-181-7
   FBA 1181
14 13 12 11 10 9 8 7 6 5 4 3 2 1

Printed in the United States of America

DEDICATION

In loving memory of Howard Fabing Twiggs and Scott Alan Bailey. I miss them.

ACKNOWLEDGMENTS

This book was written with the assistance of many dear friends and former students. First and foremost, I must thank my mentor and friend, Mark Mandell. Mark is a superb trial lawyer from Providence, Rhode Island. He encouraged me to write this book and provided much of the material herein. I only hope that I've done his brilliant ideas justice.

I am also grateful to Jim Lees of Charleston, West Virginia; Greg Cusimano of Gadsden, Alabama; and David Wenner of Phoenix, Arizona. I and countless other lawyers have learned much from their teaching. I have also been blessed with wonderful friends and colleagues like Tom Comerford and Cliff Britt of Winston-Salem, North Carolina, who have generously lent their time and considerable talents to both me and my students over the last several years.

I am deeply indebted to Professor John Petrocelli, a brilliant young scholar who teaches in the psychology department at Wake Forest University. When I began this book, I knew nothing about psychology. John's vast knowledge of the subject and patient guidance made him an invaluable resource. He not only knew the answer to my every question, he could cite the original source for the proposition from memory.

I must also thank Charles Hoogland, a delightful psychology graduate student at Wake Forest, who supplemented my research and carefully edited rough drafts of each chapter for accuracy. Several of my favorite former students made significant contributions to this work as well—Randy Ivie, Jason Walters, Heidi Perlman, Nancy Rapp, Justin Brown, Toni Grace, Jessica Schulte, Stephanie Lemos, Ryan Ames, and the late Scott Bailey. I offer my heartfelt thanks to you all.

CONTENTS

CHAPTER THREE. MEMORY

CHAPTER SIX. SOCIAL BIASES: ATTRIBUTION THEORY

CHAPTER SEVEN. CULTURAL NORMS AND BIASES

CHAPTER ONE

INTRODUCTION

"There is no neutral, 'value-free way' of presenting people with information,"[1]
nor, we might add, is there a neutral, value-free way of receiving it.

This book is designed to help lawyers try cases better. It is written for those of us who have grappled with juries and come away wondering why we lost a case we should have won. The fact that good lawyers are losing good cases with regularity suggests there may be something fundamentally wrong with our approach to trial. Although we can justify our losses by claiming that our jurors "disregarded the evidence," it is more likely that we disregarded the jurors by failing to consider what they needed and wanted to hear about the case to decide in our client's favor.

There are many factors, both conscious and unconscious, that affect the jurors' ability to make wise and rational decisions. Although we'd like to presume that law, logic, and reason will ultimately prevail, it's virtually impossible for jurors to divorce instinct and emotion from decision-making. They, like all people, bring a wealth of deeply ingrained biases, life experiences, and unrelated information to bear on every decision they make, although they're generally unaware of doing so.

To forecast how our jurors are likely to perceive, process, and remember the evidence, we need to understand how human perception, information processing, and memory operate. Jurors will inevitably rely on the same cognitive tools at trial that they normally use to solve problems and make decisions in their everyday lives. If we can learn to navigate the minefield of juror thinking, we can start winning more of the cases we deserve to win.

By extrapolating from the research of psychologists and other social scientists, we can learn to apply the basic precepts of human decision-making and information processing to the trial forum. If we factor the jurors' beliefs, biases, and information-processing strategies into our trial strategy, we can

---

1.   Jon Gertner, *Why Isn't the Brain Green?*, N.Y. TIMES MAG., April 19, 2009, at MM 36, 43 (*quoting* Elke Weber).

effectively counteract many of the unconscious thinking errors that can often skew jurors' perceptions of our case.

I. The Hierarchy of Decision-Making

Recent advances in medicine, social science, and psychology have made it possible for us to understand and confront the inherent fallibility of human decision-making. We now know that everyone uses the same basic cognitive processes to interpret and evaluate new information; therefore, we can make several broad assumptions about decision-making that help us predict how jurors are likely to perceive our case. Their responses to the evidence may surprise and confound us.

All human beings make decisions both consciously and unconsciously. Often, it's a matter of pure cognitive efficiency. We also tend to process new information through the filter of our own core values and life experiences—a tendency that leads jurors to unconsciously project their own personal biases and preconceived notions onto the evidence presented at trial.

Jurors may find certain decisions more innately compelling than others for reasons they neither understand nor appreciate. They, like all of us, may believe they're "reasoning" when they're actually "rationalizing" about how to reconcile their strongly held beliefs and emotional commitments with new conflicting information. Such behavior isn't necessarily "irrational" because it "doesn't make sense to discard an entire belief system, built up over a lifetime, because of some new snippet of information."[2]

If we can learn what compels jurors to make decisions, particularly on an unconscious level, we can fairly and professionally influence them on a much deeper level than before. Because people tend to make decisions in a hierarchical fashion, we can deduce what a "hierarchy of juror decision-making" should look like.[3] This "hierarchy" is not a scientific characterization; rather, it is based on years of preparing and trying cases and teaching others to do so. It's helpful to consider each of the "levels" of this proposed "hierarchy of decision-making" in preparing for trial.

The lowest levels of our hierarchy (Levels One and Two) are the most compelling decision-making factors because they deal with matters of personal safety. These types of decisions have the greatest potential to unfairly affect juror decision-making—without juror awareness.[4] The intermediate levels (Levels Three and Four) encompass decisions that are affected by the

---

2. *The Last Word: Made-Up Minds,* THE WEEK 48–49 (May 20, 2011). The "confirmation bias" will be discussed in more depth in chapter five.
3. This hierarchy is similar to Maslow's Hierarchical Pyramid discussed in chapter three.
4. Norbert L. Kerr et al., *Bias in Judgment: Comparing Individuals and Groups,* 103 PSYCHOL. REV. 687, 687–89 (1996).

jurors' core values and beliefs, some that are cultural or societal and others that are individual. Level Five, the highest level of decision-making, is logic and reason, which all of us employ far less frequently than we might imagine.

A. Level One: Real or Imagined Threats to Survival

Whenever jurors perceive a threat to their survival, whether real or imagined, they immediately and instinctively react by trying to protect themselves from harm. All human beings are equipped with the ability to react to threats in a matter of milliseconds—a response that can be detected with an EEG long before we're consciously aware of it.[5] This shouldn't surprise us because "[e]volution required us to react very quickly to stimuli in our environment in order to survive . . . . [Interestingly, w]e apply fight-or-flight reflexes not only to predators but to data itself."[6] In other words, our basic survival skills cause us to flee not only from potential predators but from threatening information as well.[7]

Jurors have very little control over this basic human survival response (the "freeze, fight, or flee" response) because their overriding concern is for their own personal safety—even when the harm that frightens them is either imaginary or affects someone else. This is why they view the facts of our case through the lens of their own primal fears and emotions.[8] They tend to feel personally threatened when they hear about bad things that have happened to other people.

For example, hearing about the plight of an injured plaintiff may lead jurors to mentally "flee" from the thought of being similarly injured. They may unconsciously try to alleviate the fear of suffering a similar fate by imagining how much better *they* would have behaved had they been in the plaintiff's situation. This response can adversely affect their perceptions of the merits of the plaintiff's claim.

B. Level Two: Belief in a Just World and Illusion of Control

All of us have a deep and abiding need to believe we live in a world where justice and goodness will always prevail: where good acts and good people will be rewarded and bad acts and bad people will be punished. This **belief in a just world** tends to manifest itself at trial by causing jurors to instinctively presume that the plaintiff must have done something "bad" simply because she was unable to protect herself from harm. They secretly believe that "good" people (like themselves) should be able to predict and control

---

5. *The Last Word, supra* note 2, at 48.
6. *Id., quoting* Arthur Lupia, a political scientist at the University of Michigan.
7. *Id.*
8. Kerr et al, *supra* note 4, at 687–89.

outcomes in a just world, a psychological tendency referred to as the **illusion of control**. Obviously, these unconscious presumptions work to the detriment of the injured plaintiff—unless we can effectively counteract them in advance.

C. Level Three: Social and Cultural Beliefs and Biases

The third level of our hierarchy encompasses the shared social and cultural beliefs, biases, and values that jurors have acquired over the course of a lifetime. Although not innate, enculturation has a powerful influence on the jurors' perceptions of the evidence, although most of them don't realize it. It's difficult for us to appreciate our own biases when they're shared by everyone around us. The peculiarly American biases regarding rugged independence, the acquisition of wealth, and personal responsibility make it more difficult for a deserving plaintiff to convince jurors that her injury should be redressed.

D. Level Four: "Heuristics"

Heuristics—the mental shortcuts or rules of thumb that we often use to make decisions more quickly and efficiently—affect almost every level of decision-making. Jurors often rely on this sort of streamlined decision-making, even when more thoughtful consideration is appropriate for the situation. Unfortunately, when jurors rely on heuristics to process and digest the evidence presented at trial, particularly if it's voluminous or complex, they're more susceptible to consistent, predictable thinking errors, which may significantly affect their perceptions of our case.

E. Level Five: Fully Engaged Cognitive Reasoning

At the very top of our hierarchy of decision-making is logic and reason. This tends to be the decision-making level of last resort. Few choices in life require such intense thought and effort; indeed, it's impossible for anyone to make every decision, large or small, at the highest level of our hierarchy because no one has unlimited cognitive resources. Jurors can't be expected to devote their full attention to every incremental decision they make about the evidence as the trial progresses. Nevertheless, whenever they rely on heuristics to process more difficult or complex information, the quality of their decision-making may be adversely affected.

II. Using the Hierarchy

Assigning blame in a civil case is not as easy for jurors as assigning blame in a criminal case, because the harm is rarely deliberate or intentional. This makes the burden of persuasion inherently more difficult. Although we want jurors to assign blame based on the reasons that we give them, they can't. They need to act for their own reasons, which are often different than ours. Our job is to empower jurors to do the "right" thing for reasons that seem "right" to them.

We can't change the way that jurors think, but we *can* change what we ask them to think about. If we understand how their minds and memories work, we can better decide which facts jurors are likely to find most persuasive and why. Ultimately, we may convince them to do the right thing, but not always by appealing to reason and logic.

We begin our journey with a discussion of perception and memory, which are the foundations of thought. We will then discuss how each of level of our "hierarchy of decision-making" is likely to affect juror thinking. Lastly, we will learn how to apply these strategies at trial, using an opening statement and closing argument as examples.

Chapter Two

Believing Is Seeing: Introduction to Perception and Information Processing in the Courtroom

"Jurors see the world not as it is but as they are.
Jurors see your case not as it is but as they are.
We see our case not as it is but as we are. All of us are biased."[1]

I. Introduction

Cases aren't decided on the facts, but on jurors' perceptions of the facts. Therefore, an effective advocate must have the ability to affect juror perceptions to affect the verdict that ultimately flows from those perceptions.

Most of us have worked hard to improve our communication skills because we know that persuasive communication is an essential component of advocacy. But the real potency of persuasion may lie in understanding how jurors are likely to perceive, process, and remember the evidence *as it is being presented* at trial. In other words, we need to know something about how jurors think, what they're likely to think about, and why.

This fundamentally basic, yet complex tool we call "thinking" can work to our advantage or disadvantage in court. We can exponentially improve the quality of our advocacy by presenting our case in a way that highlights or deflates the inferences and conclusions that jurors are likely to make about the evidence, based either on their past experiences or the ease with which they can remember, imagine, or recall similar instances.

Psychologists and other social scientists have studied how our brains perceive, process, and remember information. Their research clearly demonstrates that human perception and memory are inherently imperfect. All of us unconsciously manipulate our perceptions and recollections to make them conform to what we already believe or want to believe is true. As a

---

1.   *See* Eric Oliver, Facts Can't Speak for Themselves 1 (2005) (paraphrasing Anais Nin). Also note that throughout this text, lawyers will be referred to as "we" and jurors as "they."

result, both perception and memory are inevitably subjective, often inaccurate, and typically self-serving.

As jurors listen to the evidence, they instinctively and unconsciously draw inferences and conclusions about the facts based on their past experiences or on how easily they can recall similar information or events. With that in mind, we should structure our proof in a way that highlights or downplays the inferences and conclusions that our particular jurors are likely to draw about our case. Obviously, this is easier said than done.

Each juror will perceive and remember the facts of our case differently; therefore, it's difficult for us to predict how multiple jurors will perceive, process, and remember those facts. Despite this, we need to be able to make some rudimentary predictive judgments about how jurors are likely to respond to the evidence because their collective perceptions and memories—however imperfect or erroneous—form the basis of every verdict.

Fortunately, psychologists tell us that there are several key psychological constructs that all human beings share. These constructs lead jurors to project their own deeply ingrained biases and preconceived notions onto the evidence they're asked to evaluate. If we can learn what these psychological constructs are and how they affect juror decision-making, we can deal with the fundamental problems of inaccurate juror perception and memory in a much more effective way than we have in the past.

Conducting focus groups is the best way to discover how prospective jurors are likely to perceive the evidence in our case. But focus groups are expensive, and not every case merits the cost. This makes it all the more important for us to understand, at least on a very basic level, how jurors are likely to think about and respond to our particular case facts. We begin to unravel the mysteries of this basic, yet complex tool we call "thinking" with a primer on perception.

II. Perception in the Courtroom

Perception, memory, and attention are the building blocks of thought.[2] Each of these building blocks is affected by a number of conscious and unconscious factors. As advocates, we need to be particularly aware of the *unconscious* factors that affect juror thinking, because this is where the real potency of persuasion may lie. These unconscious factors comprise the lower levels of our hierarchy of decision-making.

Perception can be roughly defined as the unconscious process by which we absorb information through our five senses and immediately try to make

---

2. ELIZABETH STYLES, ATTENTION, PERCEPTION AND MEMORY: AN INTEGRATED INTRODUCTION (2005).

sense of it. **Social perception** deals with how we use that information to understand other people and make judgments about them and their behavior. (Social perception will be discussed in greater detail in chapter five on attributional biases.)

A. Moving from Perception to Recognition

At the moment of perception, we immediately and unconsciously try to categorize what we've perceived to make sense of it. Because we cannot process our perceptions in a vacuum, we must essentially "translate" or decode our perceptions to understand what they mean, at least to us. This is how we move from perception to **recognition**.

The process of moving from perception to recognition is influenced by a variety of things: (1) our life experiences, (2) our personalities, (3) the culture in which we were reared, (4) our expectations, (5) our motivations, and (6) the context in which something is perceived.[3] These perceptual predispositions have a powerful influence on our thoughts and decisions, and there is little we can do to change this.

To process our perceptions more efficiently, we rely heavily on **heuristics**, which, as we saw earlier, are mental shortcuts or general rules of thumb. In so doing, we unconsciously manipulate our perceptions to make them conform to what we expect and hope to see.[4] We also tend to remember only those perceptions that confirm to what we already believe or want to believe is true about the world and everyone in it.[5] (This fourth level of our hierarchy is discussed in chapter eight).

This is why two people may perceive the same information or event, yet react to it quite differently. More importantly for our purposes, this is why two jurors can see and hear the same evidence, yet have entirely different perceptions of the "facts." Since jurors are completely oblivious of moving from perception to recognition, they're equally oblivious to their own misperceptions in the process. This makes it difficult for them to understand why other jurors may have perceived the same information differently.[6]

Psychologist Kurt Lewin first made the distinction between the psychological environment that surrounds each of us and the non-psychological world in which objective reality exists. We can never escape our subjective

---

3. SUSAN T. FISKE, SOCIAL BEINGS: CORE MOTIVES IN SOCIAL PSYCHOLOGY (2010).
4. THOMAS GILOVICH, HOW WE KNOW WHAT ISN'T SO: THE FALLIBILITY OF HUMAN REASON IN EVERYDAY LIFE (paperback ed. 1993).
5. IRVING KIRSCH, HOW EXPECTANCIES SHAPE EXPERIENCE (1999).
6. GILOVICH, *supra* note 4; Charles G. Lord et al, *Biased Assimilation and Attitude Polarization: The Effects of Prior Theories on Subsequently Considered Evidence,* 37 J. PERSONALITY & SOCIAL PSYCHOL. 2098 (1979).

psychological environment; therefore, we can't always distinguish between subjective and objective reality.[7]

Each juror's perceptions of the evidence will be influenced by a host of variables such as personal experience, sensory capacity, gender, age, race, ethnicity, culture, family, politics, religion, intelligence, and education (the beliefs and biases that comprise the third level of our hierarchy). Therefore, we must be aware that even the most honest, well-intentioned juror will unconsciously manipulate her perceptions to make them fit neatly into her own concept of "reality" and how things ought to be. Consequently, "facts," at their core, are little more than the intensely personal, inevitably subjective, and occasionally impaired perceptions of one individual.

B. Perceiving Versus Experiencing "Facts"

We not only *perceive* the world in our own unique way: we also *experience* it differently. After practicing client-centered counseling for forty-six years, psychotherapist Carl Rogers learned that the way in which people experience an event determines how they will respond to it. Rogers concluded that our thoughts, feelings, and behaviors are a function of three things: (1) our own unique and subjective life experiences; (2) how we perceive and categorize these experiences in our minds; and (3) how we perceive ourselves.[8]

Personality, sensory capacity, and individual differences also help to explain why we perceive and experience life so differently. For example, a color-blind person may look at an apple tree and see nothing but green apples and green leaves, while most of us see bright red apples nestled among the green leaves. Some of us may like the sound of country music or the taste of raw tuna; however, we should not be surprised to find that others don't share these perceptual predispositions.

At trial, we expect multiple jurors to draw the same conclusions about the evidence. However, this is unlikely to happen because each juror perceives, interprets, and experiences the evidence differently. As a result, it may be difficult for jurors to agree on what the "true facts" of the case really are.

"Facts" are inherently difficult to identify or define, given how our minds work. Nevertheless, facts remain the hard currency of the courtroom. The Rules of Evidence generally require that our proof be factual with few exceptions—notably, expert and lay witness opinions. Deciding which facts to present and how to properly frame and sequence them becomes a much

---

7. Kurt Lewin, Principles of Topological Psychology (1936); Kurt Lewin, *Field Theory in Social Science* in Selected Theoretical Papers (D. Cartwright, ed. 1951).
8. Carl R. Rogers, Client-Centered Therapy: Its Current Practice, Implications and Theory (1951); Carl R. Rogers, *In Retrospect: Forty-Six Years,* J. Am. Psychol. 115–23 (1974).

more complex undertaking when we consider that although each juror will *receive* the same information, not all of them will *interpret* it in the same way.

For example, the juror who is a stock broker may interpret the evidence in a securities fraud case quite differently than the social worker on the panel. Similarly, a female nurse's view of a medical negligence case is unlikely to mirror that of a male motorcycle salesman, particularly since male jurors tend to have a different perspective on risky behaviors than female jurors. Our job is to try to predict, based on very limited information, how the jurors' varying interpretations of the evidence will affect our case.

We can glean insight into how jurors in a particular community are likely to interpret the evidence by conducting focus groups, either on our own or with the help of a jury consultant. Jury questionnaires are also helpful since jurors tend to be more honest on paper than in public. But the limited amount of time we have in voir dire to talk to jurors is rarely sufficient to elicit the sort of information we need to try our case because most of them are reluctant to discuss their biases, beliefs, and opinions in a public forum.

C. Resisting Persuasion

All of us tend to be resistant to persuasion—or so-called **social influence attempts**—because of the unique way in which we perceive and interpret information.[9] Our opinions are our own, and we cherish them. As the old adage says, "A man convinced against his will is of the same opinion still."[10]

Jurors are no different. If our evidence challenges their core values or beliefs, we're unlikely to be able to persuade them to change their thinking.[11]

As soon as the trial begins, each juror instinctively starts to evaluate incoming sensory data (the evidence) by making conscious and unconscious decisions about the credibility and importance of the data. Seeing, hearing, and evaluating are not separate and exclusive mental processes: they're inextricably linked and basically occur simultaneously.[12] This is why jurors find

---

9. JACK W. BREHM, A THEORY OF PSYCHOLOGICAL REACTANCE (1966).
10. Paraphrasing Samuel Butler's poem *Hudibras: The Third and Last Part,* ll. 547–50 (1694), which reads, "He that complies against his will / Is of his own opinion still."
11. *See, e.g.,* Eric S. Knowles & Jay A. Linn, *Approach-Avoidance Model of Persuasion: Alpha and Omega Strategies, in* RESISTANCE & PERSUASION, 117–48 (Eric S. Knowles & Jay A. Linn, eds. 2004); John V. Petrocelli et al, *Unpacking Attitude Certainty: Attitude Clarity and Attitude Correctness,* 92 J. PERSONALITY & SOC. PSYCHOL. 30 (2007).
12. David Brooks, *The Emotions of Reason and Morality,* WINSTON-SALEM JOURNAL, Apr. 9, 2009, at A7. *See also* D. Carlston, *Impression Formation and the Modular Mind: The Associated Systems Theory, in* THE CONSTRUCTION OF SOCIAL JUDGMENTS 301 (Leonard L. Martin & Abraham Tesser, eds. 1992) (postulating that the different forms of information we take in about a person—e.g., appearance, social status, traits, observations, relationships, evaluations, behavioral responses, orientations, affect, etc.—are represented simultaneously in memory. They are differentially reflected in reported impressions, judgments, and behavior).

it inherently difficult to remain open-minded for very long. Since many of their qualitative judgments are made prematurely without conscious thought or proper context, the potential for error is enormous.[13]

The jurors' initial perceptions of the evidence, the litigants, and the lawyers, however inaccurate, are very influential because they're extremely resistant to change. Even when jurors make a conscious effort to change their perceptions or attitudes about something, old attitudes remain in memory and continue to influence their subsequent judgments and behavior.[14] Consequently, jurors are probably going to believe the same things at the end of the trial that they believed at the beginning. But all is not lost. We can adapt our trial strategy to account for their likely perceptions of and reactions to the evidence.

D. Linking to Juror Knowledge and Beliefs to Overcome Resistance

Psychological research clearly demonstrates that there are always gaps, inaccuracies, and ambiguities in our perceptions, which we instinctively reconcile by drawing inferences and conclusions culled from our own knowledge and experience. If we're unable to **link** or mentally connect our perceptions to something familiar—something we already know, remember, or firmly believe—we're likely to do one of two things: (1) we may simply fail to process those perceptions; that is, we may completely disregard them; or (2) we may unconsciously alter those perceptions to make them conform to what we presently believe or wish to believe.

This tells us that if jurors are unable to link their perceptions of a critical piece of evidence to something familiar—something they already know or believe is true—they're likely to either disregard the offending evidence or alter it to make it conform to their preexisting beliefs and biases. We can prevent this from happening by leaving no significant gaps in our evidence. Every evidentiary gap is an invitation for jurors to fill in what they don't know or weren't told with their own inferences, interpretations, and personal biases, which inevitably distorts their perceptions of our case.

For example, a juror who has no children may presume that a stay-at-home mother has little to do other than watch her children and keep them safe from harm. If we represent a mother whose toddler was bitten in her own back yard by a neighbor's dog, we'll need to present evidence that not only proves the defendant dog owner's negligence, but our client's *lack of* negligence as well. Otherwise, the juror may fill this evidentiary gap with personal assumptions about what the mother could have and should have

---

13. Daniel T. Gilbert et al, *When Comparisons Arise,* 69 J. PERSONALITY & SOC. PSYCHOL. 227–36 (1995).
14. Richard E. Petty et al, *Implicit Ambivalence from Attitude Change: An Exploration of the PAST Model,* 90 J. PERSONALITY & SOC. PSYCHOL. 21–41 (2006).

done to prevent her child's injury. This may lead the juror to hold the mother responsible rather than the dog's owner to reconcile his own beliefs and biases with the facts of the case.

III. Decision Foundations: Information Processing and Reasoning in the Courtroom

All of us make decisions for reasons we don't fully understand because many information-processing strategies operate beyond the level of human awareness. Even though we're oblivious to their operation, these cognitive processes not only influence our thinking and how we view the world, they can also pose serious obstacles to wise and rational decision-making.

Although we may generically (and incorrectly) refer to these mental processes as either "conscious" or "unconscious,"[15] psychologists have designed **dual-processing theories** to describe two distinct ways of characterizing how people process information: (1) automatic processing (also known as "heuristic" processing and (2) controlled processing (also known as systematic processing).[16] Each is uniquely suited for different kinds of mental tasks, although in practice, they are not always used appropriately.

Particular methods of processing can lead to different judgments and conclusions about the world and sometimes to **thinking errors**[17] or mistakes in judgment. As advocates, we need to recognize how and when jurors are likely to fall prey to "automatic" (unconscious) thinking errors. This allows us to either minimize their potential damage or figure out how to use these thinking errors to our advantage to achieve a just result.

A. Automatic Processing

Automatic (or **heuristic**) **processing** is what some psychologists refer to as the **unconscious mind**. It encompasses the cognitive processes that occur beyond our level of awareness. Automatic processing is the brain's "auto pilot." It's roughly the mental equivalent of the body's autonomic functions, such as breathing or blinking our eyes. All levels of our hierarchy of decision-making except the fifth or top level (cognitive reasoning) rely on automatic processing to some extent. Generally, the lower the level, the greater the reliance on automatic processing.

---

15.   The terms "unconscious" and "subconscious" are rarely used in psychological literature today. They have been replaced with the terms "automatic" or "beyond our level of awareness." "Controlled" mental processes are the complete opposite. They are synonymous with conscious and deliberate thought.

16.   Shelley Chaiken & Yaacov Trope, Dual-Process Theories in Social Psychology (1999).

17.   Steven J. Sherman et al, *Social Cognition*, 40 Ann. Rev. Psychol. 281 (1989); Susan T. Fiske & Shelley E. Taylor, Social Cognition (2d ed. 1991).

Automatic processing runs incessantly in the background of our mind, even though we're unaware of it. It speeds information processing because it requires minimal mental effort. For example, whenever we're driving, we instantly recognize a red traffic light and come to a stop without thinking much about it. This is an "automatic" response.

All human beings are cognitive misers to some extent because our cognitive resources are limited. It would be impossible for us to consciously consider each of our sensory perceptions all the time, therefore, we instinctively preserve our "mental capital" by relying on automatic processing whenever possible because it's so fast and effortless.[18]

Automatic processing has four salient characteristics: (1) we're unaware of it; (2) we cannot control it; (3) we use it unintentionally; and (4) it is cognitively efficient because it requires minimal thought or effort.[19] Because automatic processing is so quick and efficient, it allows us to absorb seemingly unlimited amounts of information by simply encoding all of our perceptions as a total, unfocused, and disorganized experience without fully distinguishing between reality and fantasy, past and present, awake and asleep.[20]

For example, if we're driving to a restaurant for dinner, we may suddenly realize we're headed in the wrong direction because we've automatically taken our usual route to work. We drive this route so frequently that we take it without thinking; therefore, we must consciously decide to take another route to reach the proper destination.

Jurors rely heavily on automatic processing because it's appropriate for the vast majority of decisions they make in a day. Most of life's decisions are simple, routine, and repetitive and don't require the use of controlled processing. As Malcolm Gladwell argued in his book *Blink*,[21] people often come to accurate judgments in the blink of an eye (automatically). Nevertheless, automatic processing is generally inappropriate for making the kinds of important decisions we ask jurors to make at trial.

Automatic processing is inherently fallible because it happens without intention and is inextricably linked to each individual's background, beliefs, and biases. This is why it so often yields flawed results. For example, some

---

18.   FISKE & TAYLOR, *supra* note 17.

19.   John A. Bargh, *The Four Horsemen of Automaticity: Awareness, Efficiency, Intention, and Control in Social Cognition, in* HANDBOOK OF SOCIAL COGNITION VOLUME 1: BASIC PROCESSES 1, 2 (Robert S. Wyer Jr. & Thomas K. Srull, eds., 2nd ed. 1994). Note that automatic and controlled processing may also be referred to as low and high levels of cognitive elaboration.

20.   Charles J. Brainerd & Valerie F. Reyna, *Fuzzy Trace Theory: Dual-Processes in Reasoning, Memory, and Cognitive Neuroscience*, 28 ADVANCES IN CHILD DEV. & BEHAV. 41 (2001); Valerie F. Reyna & Charles J. Brainerd, *Fuzzy-Trace Theory: An Interim Synthesis*, 7 LEARNING & INDIVIDUAL DIFFERENCES 1 (1995).

21.   MALCOLM GLADWELL, BLINK: THE POWER OF THINKING WITHOUT THINKING (2005).

jurors may believe that a witness who wears a uniform is more likely to tell the truth than a witness in civilian clothing because the uniform itself conveys a certain expertise. These jurors may automatically give more weight to the testimony of a law enforcement officer, a nurse, or a soldier without being consciously aware of what they're doing.

B. Controlled Processing

Controlled (or systematic) processing is the opposite of automatic processing. It is at the top of our hierarchy of decision-making. Controlled processing requires effort and concentration. It's the mental processing function we use to engage in abstract or conceptual reasoning. It helps us organize and interpret information in a logical, deliberate manner. We use controlled processing when studying for a test or preparing for trial. **Dual processing** occurs whenever we use automatic and controlled processing simultaneously or alternate back and forth between the two.

Most intelligent, highly motivated people actually enjoy controlled processing and cognitive exertion. They tend to rely on controlled processing whenever they process new information because they have a **high need for cognition**. Conversely, people with a **low need for cognition** simply don't enjoy intense, sustained concentration.[22] They prefer to make decisions quickly and intuitively and move on rather than search for the perfect answer or outcome. In other words, they instinctively seek **cognitive closure**.

It's reasonable to expect that jurors with a low need for cognition will tend to rely on automatic processing more often than those with a high need for cognition. This speeds their decision-making, but it also increases the number of thinking errors they're likely to make. Automatic processing may invite the jurors to come to one conclusion despite the fact that the evidence suggests another. (However, there is some research to suggest that thinking too deeply about information can also lead to thinking errors.[23])

Obviously, we want jurors to consider the evidence deliberately and carefully before making a decision. When they fail to pay close attention to important information, they're less likely to recall it completely or accurately. In other words, when jurors ignore or selectively attend to critical information (which all of them do at one time or another), they're more prone to make thinking errors.

To minimize the number of juror thinking errors, we should present the most important evidence in a variety of ways that will address both

---

22. John T. Cacioppo & Richard E. Petty, *The Need for Cognition*, 42 J. PERSONALITY & SOC. PSYCHOL. 116, 130 (1982).

23. Zakary L. Tormala et al, *Ease of Retrieval Effects in Persuasion: A Self-Validation Analysis*, 28 J. PERSONALITY & SOC. PSYCHOL. BULL. 1700–12 (2002).

automatic and controlled processing. Appropriately emphasizing and repeating our key points helps jurors process the evidence more effectively and ensures that our message will reach all of the jurors, each of whom may be using one or a combination of these types of processing at various intervals during trial.

C. Motivated Reasoning

There are many ways to categorize the process of "reasoning," which is defined as the process by which we generate and evaluate arguments in our minds and reach conclusions about them.[24] There are many different types or categories of reasoning, all of which are at the top of our hierarchy of decision-making. Most of us are familiar with **deductive and inductive reasoning**. Deductive reasoning roughly involves taking specific examples and drawing conclusions or generalizations from them, while inductive reasoning is just the opposite. More important for our purposes, however, is another type of reasoning: **motivated reasoning**.

Studies show that if we think our decision will be (1) significant, (2) irreversible, and (3) that we'll be held personally accountable for it, we will invest greater time and effort in trying to reach an accurate result. Obviously, we want to encourage jurors to use motivated reasoning at trial because it tends to yield decisions that are relatively free of bias or personal motivation.[25] However, if the above components are lacking, jurors are more prone to make quite rudimentary decisions based on their personal goals and motives,[26] despite the fact that they're supposed to be impartial and unbiased. Therefore, it's important for us to encourage jurors to give the evidence the careful consideration that it deserves. We can encourage the use of motivated reasoning and controlled processing by telling jurors how important their decision is to us, our client, and the community at the beginning of voir dire:

> This case is very important to my client, Susan Miller. She has just one chance to come to court and have her case decided by members of her community. As her lawyer, it's my job to be sure that everyone who sits on this jury will try to be fair to Ms. Miller. [Jurors don't really believe us if we ask them to be fair to both sides.] Mr. Jones, can you promise us that you'll do your best to be fair to Ms. Miller?

---

24. Douglas A. Bernstein et al, Psychology 290 (8th ed. 2008).
25. Daniel W. McAllister et al, *The Contingency Model for the Selection of Decision Strategies: An Empirical Test of the Effects of Significance, Accountability, and Reversibility,* 24 Org. Behav. & Human Decision Processes, 228–44 (1979).
26. *Id.*

This approach emphasizes the importance of the case and the fact that it can't be tried twice.

At the beginning of our closing argument, we should reiterate the importance of the jurors' decision. We should also warn them that they will be required to justify their positions on the evidence to their fellow jurors during deliberations:[27]

> There are two places in this great country of ours where good citizens like you can make a significant difference: the ballot box and the jury box. You have a very important job to do today, and I'm confident you'll do it well.
>
> At the end of this trial, the judge will instruct you to go back to the jury room and pick a foreperson. Part of the foreperson's job is to be sure than each and every one of you has an opportunity to express your opinions about the evidence and tell your fellow jurors what you think a just result should be.

Most jurors are nervous about public speaking, so they'll try to pay closer attention to the evidence to avoid embarrassing themselves in the jury room when it's their turn to speak. This also encourages jurors to hold one another accountable for the promises they made during voir dire.

IV. Helping Jurors Process Information Appropriately

Jurors will make many decisions automatically, despite our best efforts to encourage controlled processing and motivated reasoning. It's simply human nature to default to the lower levels of the hierarchy of decision-making because so little cognitive effort is required.

Luckily, we can adjust to this reality because automatic processing yields relatively predictable biases and thinking errors. We can reduce the adverse effects of improper automatic processing by linking our case to the jurors' own beliefs and biases. If we couple what we know about their backgrounds and life experiences with a basic understanding of how their minds and memories work, we can do a reasonably good job of predicting the best and most persuasive way to present our evidence. In other words, we can harness the predictable biases and thinking errors caused by automatic processing to achieve a just result for our client, even when jurors make decisions at the lowest level of our hierarchy of decision-making.

In the chapters that follow, we will explore several other important thinking strategies that jurors commonly use to process the information presented at trial. We begin by learning how memory works. We then discuss why and

---

27. Ziva Kunda, *The Case for Motivated Reasoning,* 108 PSYCHOL. BULL. 480–98 (1990).

how jurors unconsciously alter their perceptions to make them conform to their strongly held beliefs and self-images. We also discuss how to structure our case in a way that maximizes the benefit or lessens the adverse impact of the predictable inferences and conclusions that jurors are likely to draw about the evidence in our case. Finally, the last chapter provides examples of how to use these techniques in the context of an actual opening statement and closing argument.

CHAPTER THREE

MEMORY

I. Introduction

The accuracy of any verdict depends on the jury's ability to understand and remember the evidence. But memory is volatile, inexact, selective, and often inaccurate. Because our orientation to life is necessarily autobiographical, we tend to remember things in distinctly personal terms; therefore, memory is also highly individualistic. In fact, **self-reference effect** research shows that we remember information better when we consider how relevant it is to our self-concept.[1] This means that what we remember and how well we remember it is inevitably a reflection of who we are, what we value most, and what our life experiences have been.

In recent decades, scientists have begun to unravel the mysteries of memory. As they've learned more about how people acquire, store, and recall information, many common information-processing tendencies have emerged. Although there are a variety of complex and often overlapping theories about how various types of memory work, the simplest approach will suffice for our purposes.

In this chapter, we will discuss a few of the basic types of memory that jurors rely on at trial. We begin with a discussion of short-term and long-term memory and conclude with suggestions on how to improve the jury's recollection of the evidence.

A. Short-Term and Long-Term Memory

Short-term or working memory stores limited amounts of information for brief periods of time. We generally hold or "maintain" information in short-term memory only long enough to **manipulate** or actually use it. Once the information has served its purpose, we usually forget it unless we

---

1. T.B. Rogers, *A Model of the Self as an Aspect of the Human Information Processing System,* in PERSONALITY, COGNITION, AND SOCIAL INTERACTION 193–214 (Nancy Cantor & John F. Kihlstrom, eds. 1981); T.B. Rogers et al, *Self-Reference and the Encoding of Personal Information,* 35 J. PERSONALITY & SOC. PSYCHOL. 677–88 (1977).

think it may be important in the future. If so, we must make a conscious effort to remember it.

For example, if we go to a restaurant for the first time and enjoy a wonderful dinner, we'll make a mental note of the entree we ordered for future reference. We'll probably forget the other items on the menu because they're simply not important to us. But if we're hired to wait tables at the restaurant, we'll need to familiarize ourselves with the regular menu and each day's specials so we can tell patrons what's available each evening. This requires conscious effort because we must transfer the information from short-term into long-term memory.

Long-term memory stores information we view as necessary or important for an extended period of time. Only a small amount of the information in working memory is actually **encoded** or transferred into long-term memory. Unless we mentally **rehearse** or repeat new information as we learn it, we'll typically forget it in about eighteen seconds[2]—a sobering prospect for trial lawyers, given that we must rely on jurors to remember the evidence to reach a just verdict.

If the amount of information we present at trial exceeds the capacity of the jurors' short-term memory, the number of juror thinking errors is likely to increase.[3] Therefore, our job is to make the jurors' job easy by helping them absorb and remember the evidence more effectively.

B. Information Overload ("Cognitive Busyness")

Trials are inherently stressful to jurors. They're inundated with large amounts of new information. They're expected to resolve conflicts for people they don't know in matters they're unfamiliar with. They're asked to apply rules they may find difficult to understand—and we don't even tell them what those rules are until the very end of the trial. Nevertheless, we expect jurors to keep pace with the evidence, even if we're doing a poor job of presenting it.

The difficulty of the jurors' mission is compounded by the fact that they're relegated to the role of mere passive listeners. They're not permitted to ask questions. They cannot request additional information nor ask that certain portions of the evidence be repeated. They can't even discuss the case among themselves until they retire to deliberate. This total lack of active involve-

---

2.   *Id.*

3.   John Brown and Lloyd and Margaret Peterson devised the "Brown-Peterson procedure" to see how long information remains in memory if rehearsal is prevented. *See* John Brown, *Some Tests of the Decay Theory of Immediate Memory,* 10 QTRLY EXPERIMENTAL PSYCHOL. 12–21 (1958).

ment makes paying close attention more difficult, particularly if the trial is lengthy.

The combination of these factors has a profound effect on juror decision-making. Many psychological studies have shown that information overload, known to psychologists as **cognitive busyness**, actually *inhibits* the accurate processing of information, particularly when conscious deliberation is required.[4] This means that jurors tend to experience "information overload" more quickly than we might imagine.

We must appreciate the difficulty of the task jurors face and respect the limits of their memories and attention spans. Creating strategies to improve the jurors' ability to absorb, process, and remember the evidence can help, but first we need a basic understanding of how memory actually works.

C. Methods of Encoding Memory

We acquire and **encode** (enter) information into memory in much the same way as we "download" information onto our computer. At trial, jurors typically encode information into memory in three different ways. **Acoustic (auditory) encoding** is a means of encoding information in a sequence of sounds, as if we're talking to ourselves.[5] **Visual encoding** operates by encoding information as pictures or images that we can actually see in our mind's eye.[6] **Semantic encoding** occurs when we rely on our general store of knowledge to interpret the meaning of new information.[7] How we encode information influences not only what we remember, but how well we remember it.

Acoustic encoding is the predominant method for transferring information into short-term memory.[8] It's also the principal method used to present evidence at trial. As jurors listen to the evidence, they immediately and unconsciously evaluate what was said and decide whether to believe, disbelieve, or disregard it. We can capitalize on this phenomenon with careful pacing and well-timed pauses that allow jurors to reflect on and assess the relative importance of what we say, which increases their capacity to remember it.

---

4. *See, e.g.,* Pierre Barrouillet et al, *Time and Cognitive Load in Working Memory,* J. Experimental Psychol.: Learning, Memory, and Cognition 33, 570–85 (2007); D.T. Gilbert & R.E. Osborne, *Thinking Backward: Some Curable and Incurable Consequences of Cognitive Busyness,* J. Personality & Soc. Psychol. 57, 940–49 (1989); G.T. Gilbert et al, *On Cognitive Busyness: When Person Perceivers Meet Persons Perceived,* J. Personality & Soc. Psychol. 54, 733–40 (1988); J. Sweller, *Cognitive Load During Problem Solving: Effects on Learning,* 12 Cognitive Science 257–85 (1988).
5. Douglas A. Bernstein et al, Psychology 246 (8th ed. 2008).
6. *Id.*
7. *Id.*
8. *Id.*

II. Schemata

Schemata (or, more informally, "schemas") are the basic cognitive frameworks we develop over the course of our lives to categorize objects, persons, places, and events in ways that help us interpret and make sense of the world around us.[9] We rely on our schemata to organize information and past experiences so that we can better understand new experiences.[10] Our schemata also determine how we encode and **reconstruct** memory.

It's helpful to think of our schemata as the mental file folders where all of our knowledge, beliefs, and expectations are organized in our brains.[11] Because it's impossible to process information in isolation, we inevitably categorize it in ways that reflect who we are, how we think, and how we view the world.

A. How We Create Schemata

We begin creating schemata as young children. Each schema comprises a unit of knowledge about a certain behavior, symbol, or mental activity.[12] As we encounter new things for the first time, we integrate the new information, activity, or concept into memory by incorporating it into our schemata.

For example, as toddlers, we might initially categorize all four-legged animals as "dogs" because our schema or mental representation for "dog" isn't yet fully developed.[13] As our "dog schema" becomes more sophisticated, we learn to tell the difference between dogs and cats. Later, we're able to distinguish one particular breed of dog from another. As we learn from our experience with dogs, the sophistication of our dog schema expands to include things like which breeds are dangerous (perhaps because they have snarled or snapped at us in the past) and which ones are safe (pets we have loved).

We also rely on our schemata to learn how to perform certain activities. For example, we learn how to button a shirt by creating a schema for pushing a button through a buttonhole. We learn how to ride a bike by creating a schema for steering and pedaling while keeping our balance. We learn to perform mental activities such as reading or multiplication by creating appropriate schemata for words and mathematical calculations.

Our schemata continue to develop and change throughout our lives. By adulthood, we've created innumerable and highly individualized schemata.

---

9. JEAN PIAGET, THE ORIGINS OF INTELLIGENCE IN CHILDREN (1952); FREDERIC BARTLETT ET AL., SCRIPTS, PLANS, GOALS AND UNDERSTANDING: AN INQUIRY INTO HUMAN KNOWLEDGE STRUCTURES (1977).
10. JEAN PIAGET, THE LANGUAGE AND THOUGHT OF THE CHILD (1959).
11. FREDERIC BARTLETT, REMEMBERING: AN EXPERIMENTAL AND SOCIAL STUDY (2d ed. 1995).
12. BERNSTEIN, *supra* note 5, at 465.
13. *Id.* at 466.

Because no two minds are identical and no two people share the same life experiences, our schemata are as unique as our DNA. This is why no two jurors perceive and remember the evidence in the same way.

Jurors have their own preconceived notions (schemata) about how particular events should unfold and how people should behave in various situations. For example, if we're involved in a medical malpractice case, jurors will come to court with certain expectations about how doctors and patients should behave. We need to know what those expectations are and how they're likely to affect juror perceptions of the evidence. In voir dire, we should ask jurors how often they visit a doctor's office; if they have a primary care physician; if they've ever visited a specialist; how they expect a physician to behave; how much time they expect the doctor to spend with them; and whether their personal experiences with physicians have been positive or negative.

We need to explore how juror schemata are likely to affect their perceptions of the evidence with pretrial focus groups, jury questionnaires, and voir dire. These tools help us develop and present evidence that shows how our client acted consistently with juror expectations and how the opposing party did not. Most jurors expect doctors to patiently listen to a patient's complaints and take time to explain their diagnoses in simple terms that their patients can easily understand. On the other hand, they expect patients to follow their doctor's orders and take their medications exactly as prescribed.

If we represent the defendant physician in a medical malpractice case, we should present evidence of how much time our client spent gathering information about the plaintiff's medical history, listening to her complaints, performing a thorough physical examination, and making sure she understood how and when to take her medication. We should also present evidence of the plaintiff's noncompliant behavior. We can show that she failed to follow our client's instructions to get plenty of rest and never purchased the medication our client prescribed for her.

All of our jurors have well-developed schemata for certain types of people, places, and things. For example, jurors who have had unpleasant experiences with "movers," "courthouses," or "lawnmowers" may react negatively to the mere mention of such because their schemata for these people and things cause them to be instinctively apprehensive. Other jurors, however, may have considerably different schemata for the same things.

As lawyers, whenever we think of a "courtroom," we have a certain mental image of what a courtroom should look like. It will probably resemble one we've spent time in. Other lawyers may not have the same mental image of a courtroom, but their general "courtroom schema" will probably resemble our own.

Jurors, however, aren't likely to share our "courtroom schema" or our "lawyer schema." Their schemata of courtrooms and lawyers have probably been shaped by television, movies, and negative publicity rather than actual experience. Therefore, their expectations of what courtrooms should look like and how lawyers should behave are quite different from ours.

The jury's "lawyer schema" is often unflattering because they've been conditioned to think of us as pompous, overbearing, and rude. We have to counteract their negative lawyer schema by always conducting ourselves in a respectful and dignified manner. We want to be viewed as the exception rather than the rule.

It's critical for us to explore how jurors' schemata are likely to affect their perceptions of the evidence. There are many tools we can use to elicit this information, such as pretrial focus groups, jury questionnaires, shadow juries, and, of course, voir dire. These tools can help us discover, develop, and present evidence that shows how our client acted consistently with juror expectations (schemata) and how the opposing party did not.

B. Accommodation and Assimilation

Whenever we encounter something new that doesn't fit into an existing schema, we have several options. First, if the disparity is too great, we may discard the new information and remember none of it. Second, if we don't have an existing schema that seems appropriate, we can construct a brand new one. This process is called **accommodation**.[14] Third, we can *make* the new information fit where it doesn't really belong by altering our perception of it. This process is called **assimilation**.[15] Once we decide where the new information, experience, or event fits best, we can react appropriately based on our past knowledge and experience.

We create new schemata at a rapid rate during childhood through the process of accommodation. This process slows over time, however, as our schemata become more complex and specialized. As adults, we unconsciously tend to opt for assimilation rather than create a new schema that more properly "accommodates" the new information. As a result, we often manipulate and distort new data by forcing it into an existing, but inappropriate schema (assimilation). In other words, we essentially squeeze a square peg into a round hole without being consciously aware that we're changing its shape. This may cause us to react to the new information inappropriately because we've erroneously categorized it in the wrong schema.

---

14. PIAGET, *supra* note 9.
15. *Id.*

C. A Disastrous Example

Nearly all of us have a Santa Claus schema. We know that Santa Claus is a big fellow who wears a red suit with white fur trim and that he's jolly, generous, and kind. Whenever our "Santa schema" is violated, however, we may be caught off guard and respond inappropriately.

Recently, a disgruntled husband dressed as Santa Claus showed up at his ex-wife's family Christmas party with a gun and opened fire on family members. Most of them were so shocked to see "Santa" firing a weapon that their reaction times were much slower than usual.[16] Some of them simply froze in fear rather than running for their lives. Consequently, they were either killed or wounded—in part because their "Santa schema" was violated. The victims could not conceive of "Santa" as a murderer, so they failed to react quickly enough to get out of harm's way.

At trial, our jurors' individual schemata define how they will evaluate the litigants and their behavior. Luckily, everyone deals with many comparable experiences in their daily lives, therefore, we and our jurors will share many of the same basic models or schemata of what a particular experience, person, or thing should look like. But if the facts of our case violate the jurors' schemata, which happens whenever an unusual or unexpected event brings us to court, jurors may easily misinterpret what happened.

For example, if our client was severely injured in a two-car accident, but neither car was damaged, we may have a hard time convincing jurors that her claim is valid. Their schema for "serious car accident" probably includes significant damage to the cars involved, which is something we'll have to explain.

If we fail to present our evidence in a way that is consistent with their schemata, jurors may fill any gaps in the evidence with their own memories and life experiences. In other words, they unconsciously "fill in the blanks" in a manner that's consistent with how their minds and memories work, which can lead to an unjust verdict. (These concepts will be elaborated on in the discussion of belief perseverance and confirmation bias, in chapter four.) To prevent this from happening, we need to know what our jury pool's relevant schemata are likely to be so that our evidence satisfies juror expectations.

---

16. Robert Dougherty, *Santa Slayings Consume Christmas Eve in California*, ASSOCIATED CONTENT: BUSINESS & FINANCE, December 27, 2008, *available at* http://www.associatedcontent.com/article/1339944/santa_slayings_consume_christmas_eve.html?cat=17.

III. The Reconstructive Nature of Memory

Remembering is a reconstructive process. Whenever we search our schemata and attempt to recall past events, experiences, or information, we actually "recreate" the memory as we bring it to mind. In other words, whenever we retrieve information from memory, we automatically **recode** or convert it from one form to another to make it readily accessible. This means that a memory is formed at the moment of perception and then reconstructed each time we recall the information.

Unfortunately, reconstructed memory is inexact, highly selective, and often inaccurate because the nature of memory is more generic than specific. We can't possibly remember all of the details that we automatically encode in our brain at the moment of perception.[17] We can usually conjure up the Cliffs Notes of a particularly vivid or important memory, but rarely are we able to retrieve a complete and unabridged account of what actually happened. As a result, our memories of past events are broad, but shallow.[18]

For example, whenever we drive a car, we don't remember every billboard and building we pass along the highway because we're focused on the road ahead. Although our brain perceives and records this peripheral sensory data automatically, it retains the data for a mere fraction of a second: just long enough for us to interpret what we've seen so we can keep our car on the road. Unless we make a concerted effort to remember something specific, our perceptions simply disappear from memory once they've served their purpose. This is how we avoid information overload.[19]

A. Explicit and Implicit Memory

Memories are recalled both intentionally and unintentionally. Whenever we make a conscious effort to remember something and are aware of doing so, we're using **explicit memory**.[20] In law school, for example, if the professor asks us a question about the day's assignment, we draw on our explicit memory of what we've read in preparation for class to give the correct answer.

Conversely, whenever we unconsciously allow our prior experiences to influence our present thinking, we're using **implicit memory**.[21] For example, if your client reminds a juror of someone he has known and disliked in the past, he may instinctively dislike your client without knowing why. Because

---

17. BARTLETT, *supra* note 11.
18. *Id.*
19. *Id.*
20. Michael E. Masson & Colin M. MacLeod, *Reenacting the route to interpretation: Enhanced perceptual identification without prior perception,* 121 J. EXPERIMENTAL PSYCHOL. 145 (1992).
21. Henry L. Roediger, *Implicit Memory: Retention without Remembering,* 45 AM. PSYCHOL. 1043 (1990).

the connection was made through implicit memory, the juror doesn't realize that he's allowing a memory of someone else to affect his opinion of your client. This is why implicit memory is referred to as "retention without remembering."[22]

Implicit memory wields enormous influence over juror decision-making because it lends the illusion of truth to certain facts, regardless of whether they're true or not—simply because these facts are consistent with something jurors may have thought or experienced in the past. Implicit memory may even lead jurors to inadvertently associate past personal knowledge or experiences with what they're presently learning about the case. Because they have no explicit memory of the original source, they cannot distinguish what they previously knew or experienced from present testimony. In other words, jurors may not be able to distinguish implicit from explicit memory.

As jurors reconstruct the evidence, they automatically fill in the holes or gaps in the evidence with their own personal "memory filler," which is comprised of inferences and conclusions drawn from their personal attitudes, beliefs, and opinions. This may cause them to confuse one memory with another or to "remember" details about people, places, things, or events that never really existed, save in their minds. As a result, what jurors believe is accurate memory may actually be little more than a **confabulation**—the combination of real memories with what is actually belief or imagination—simply because it seems to fill the gap (in their memory or in the evidence) so perfectly.[23] Although this "memory filler" may be invented, imagined, or inaccurate, jurors nevertheless accept it as true—simply because it's consistent with their other, more accurate memories of the evidence.[24]

In addition, the more vivid the imagined memory, the more likely jurors are to believe it actually occurred. This is a phenomenon known as **imagination inflation**.[25] As a result, each juror's own life experiences, values, and biases not only affect their perceptions of the evidence as it unfolds, these factors may also affect subsequent retrievals of the evidence from memory. This creates a veritable algorithm for unconscious juror thinking errors.

---

22. *Id.*
23. German E. Berrios, *Confabulations: A Conceptual History*, 7 J. HISTORY OF THE NEUROSCIENCES 225–41 (1999).
24. Elizabeth Loftus & John Palmer, *Reconstruction of Automatic Destruction: An Example of the Interaction between Language and Memory*, 13 J. VERBAL LEARNING & VERBAL BEHAV. 585 (1974); ELIZABETH LOFTUS, MEMORY: SURPRISING NEW INSIGHTS INTO HOW WE REMEMBER AND WHY WE FORGET (1980).
25. Maryanne Garry & Devon L. Polaschek, *Imagination and Memory*, 9 CURRENT DIRECTIONS PSYCHOL. SCI. 6–10 (2000).

B. Schemata and Memory Contamination

Closely related to implicit memory is memory contamination. Because each of our memories is placed in "collective storage" and organized into a myriad of "mental file folders" within our schemata, some memories will inevitably intermingle with one another.[26]

This occurs because we're constantly reconstructing, using, and re-filing memories from our schemata. In the process, we occasionally make mistakes. We may inadvertently misfile a memory in the wrong mental file folder without ever realizing our error.[27] Once the memory enters the tangled "memory network" of our mind, however, we can no longer distinguish between the original memory and the misfiled memory. Over time, we may misfile thousands of memories in the wrong place, which inevitably leads to confusion. This is how we inadvertently **contaminate** memory.

As jurors listen to the evidence, they immediately try to categorize the new information into the proper mental file folders. Because their schemata have inevitably been contaminated over the years, contamination of memory may occur and recur during trial as jurors continue filing new information into appropriate, and perhaps inappropriate, mental file folders. This can exponentially increase the possibilities for juror error.

C. An Example of Inaccurate Memory Reconstruction

One of the most famous experiments on the reconstructive nature of memory and how easily it can be contaminated was conducted by Elizabeth Loftus and John Palmer in 1974. Participants watched seven different film clips of a traffic accident. Later, some of them were asked how fast the cars were traveling when they "smashed" into each other. Others were asked how fast the cars were traveling when they "hit" each other. When remembering the accident, participants offered faster estimates of speed in response to the word "smashed" rather than "hit."[28] Merely changing one word in the question had a significant effect on how they reconstructed the event from memory.

In a second experiment, participants were asked how fast the cars were going when they "smashed," "collided," "bumped," "hit," or "contacted" each

---

26. John D. Bransford & Jeffery J. Franks, *The Abstraction of Linguistic Ideas,* 2 Cognitive Psychol. 331 (1971) (explaining that memories aren't stored separately).

27. Bartlett, *supra* note 11; William Brewer & James C. Treyens, *Role of Schemata in Memory for Places,* 13 Cognitive Psychol. 207 (1981). Schemata, along with concepts, propositions, images, mental models, memory scripts, and cognitive maps, comprise the ingredients of thought.

28. Elizabeth Loftus, Memory, *supra* note 24.

other. Estimates of speed changed from fastest for "smashed" to slowest for "contacted" with each successive word change.[29]

Next, Loftus and Palmer implanted a false fact by asking participants if they remembered seeing broken glass at the scene of the accident when, in fact, there was none. Participants who reconstructed the event when the verb "smashed" was used actually recalled having seen the glass, although it was not in the film.[30] These experiments demonstrate how the wording and framing of questions can actually alter the content of juror memory by embedding false information through the power of suggestion.

D. Interference

Interference is the process through which the storage or retrieval of information is impaired by the presence of other information.[31] **Retroactive interference** occurs whenever we put new information in memory that interferes with our ability to recall older information already stored there.[32] For example, if we look up a phone number, then look at the charges on our credit card bill before dialing it, the phone number is likely to be displaced in short-term memory by the "interference" of the dollar amounts on our credit card statement. As a result, we may remember the digits in the telephone number in the wrong order or forget them entirely.

Retroactive interference may occur during jury deliberations when jurors compare and contrast their own memories of the evidence with those of their fellow jurors.[33] One juror's inaccurate memory of the evidence may "interfere" with another juror's accurate memory. A juror may actually *alter* the content of her own memory to conform to that of the majority, presuming everyone else simply can't be wrong.[34]

Proactive interference occurs when old information that we've learned in the past interferes with our ability to learn or recall new information.[35] This

---

29. *Id.*
30. *Id.*
31. BERNSTEIN, *supra* note 5, at 262–63.
32. *Id.* at 263. Geoffrey Keppel & Benton J. Underwood, *Retroactive Inhibition of R-S Associations,* 64 J. VERBAL LEARNING & BEHAV. 400–04 (1962). In a recent study, two groups of participants memorized nonsense words. One group memorized the words in the morning and were tested on their ability to recall the words eight to twelve hours later. This group did not recall the nonsense words as well as the group who learned the words at night, went to bed, and were tested the next morning. No intervening perceptions interfered with their earlier memory since they only slept in the interim. John G. Jenkins & Karl M. Dallenback, *Oblivescence During Sleep and Waking,* 35 AM. J. PSYCHOL. 605 (1924).
33. Nancy Pennington & Reid Hastie, *Explanation-Based Decision-Making: Effects of Memory Structure on Judgment,* 14 J. EXPER. PSYCHOL.: LEARNING, MEMORY & COGNITION 521 (1988).
34. *Id. See* chapter six on culture codes and social compliance.
35. BERNSTEIN, *supra* note 5 at 264.

is the opposite of retroactive interference where new information is the interfering information. If, for example, we look up a new phone number, we may easily confuse it with an older phone number already stored in memory. Proactive interference can be a recurring problem at trial because of the vast amount of new information jurors are asked to remember. It's easy for them to confuse their past memories with what they're presently learning about our case.

Many other things can interfere with the quality of memory, such as mental acuity, rest, and time of day.[36] The jury's level of attention also has a profound effect on what they remember and how well they remember it. (Keeping the jury's attention has received extensive coverage in the literature, so we don't deal with it here.)

Paring our case down to its essential facts prevents relatively unimportant information from interfering with more important information. This is but one of many reasons that our presentation of evidence should be simple, straightforward, and succinct.

E. The Truth About Memory

At trial, we may naively expect jurors—total strangers to the underlying event—to fully understand and accurately remember the testimony of witnesses, the content of documents and other exhibits, and the judge's instructions on the law. As we can see, however, the processes of memory work against this expectation.

Jurors process information in ways that are consistent with who they are and what they believe. This leads them to accept and remember evidence that is consistent with what they believed before the trial began and to reject, revise, or forget evidence that is inconsistent with their beliefs and self-concepts. All of these factors contribute to the jurors' unwarranted confidence in what may actually be inaccurate memory.

The root of the problem is our imperfect mental filing system. New information often interferes with older information, which makes "cross-pollination" of old and new memories nearly inevitable. This is why jurors may inadvertently make assumptions and inferences about the evidence that are incorrect. Unfortunately, what they *think* they know and what the evidence actually shows may be two different things since memory is, in the final analysis, more figurative than literal.

---

36. Pierre Barrouilet et al, *Time Constraints and Resource Sharing in Adults' Working Memory Spans,* 133(1) J. EXPER. PSYCHOL.: GEN. 83–100 (Mar. 2004).

IV. Ways to Improve Juror Memory

Despite the inherent fallibility of memory, there are strategies we can use to improve the jurors' ability to understand and remember the evidence. Several of these strategies are outlined below.

A. The Serial Position Effect

Our ability to recall information is partially determined by its placement in a sequence, a phenomenon called the **serial position effect**.[37] Because of this well-documented psychological phenomenon, the way in which we order our proof has a significant impact on how jurors view the evidence. They give disproportionate weight to evidence presented first and last, tendencies known as the **primacy and recency effects**.[38]

1. The Primacy Effect

Most of us are able to recall the information we hear first in a particular sequence (**the primacy effect**[39]) for two reasons: (1) our minds are more keenly attuned to the absorption of information at the beginning of a task; and (2) what we hear first remains in working memory longer than information presented later. Therefore, the information is more likely to be transferred to long-term memory where it can be remembered and retrieved later.[40]

Jurors typically pay closer attention at the beginning of trial when their minds are fresh and we have their full attention. They're also more likely to remember information presented at the beginning of each day of trial and after each recess (with the notable exception of the lunch recess) because they've had a chance to rest and refresh their minds.

The primacy effect is most influential when people are asked to evaluate opposite sides of a controversial issue, particularly if both sides are presented within a week's time.[41] This means that the primacy effect will have a more

---

37. The serial position effect, formerly known as "serial recall," is the oldest memory paradigm. It was designed by German psychologist Hermann Ebbinghaus in his treatise, MEMORY: A CONTRIBUTION TO EXPERIMENTAL PSYCHOLOGY (1885), which was translated from German to English in 1913.
38. The concepts of primacy and recency were introduced by Richard C. Atkinson and Richard M. Shiffrin in their article, *Human Memory: A Proposed System and its Control Processes, in* THE PSYCHOLOGY OF LEARNING AND MOTIVATION II (Kenneth W. Spence & Janet T. Spence eds. 1968).
39. *Id.*
40. *Id.*
41. Norman Miller & Donald Campbell, *Recency and Primacy in Persuasion as a Function of the Timing of Speeches and Measurements,* 59 J. ABNORMAL & SOC. PSYCHOL. 1–9 (1959).

significant effect on juror memory and decision-making than recency, unless the trial is lengthy.[42]

Our ability to influence juror decision-making peaks at the beginning of trial then quickly diminishes over time; therefore, it's essential that we structure our evidence to account for this strong propensity. We should structure our case so that important evidence is presented when jurors are most likely to be attentive. Primacy should also affect the order of witnesses. For example, we should be wary of calling an expert out of order merely to accommodate his busy schedule. It's much more important for us to accommodate the way in which jurors absorb and remember the evidence. Creating "new beginnings" and "visible conclusions" within the trial itself and within the testimony of each witness signals to jurors when we're about to change topics, which encourages them to pay closer attention.

For example, if we begin each morning of trial with our most important and compelling evidence and conclude that particular topic before the morning recess, we've actually **primed** or subconsciously prepared, jurors to pay closer attention to what matters most.[43] If we repeat this process immediately before each recess and at the end of each day of trial, jurors will look forward to hearing what comes next.

2. Primacy and Juror "Trial Stories"

> *There are only two or three human stories, and they go on repeating themselves as fiercely as if they had never happened before . . . .*[44]
>
> Willa Cather

As soon as the trial begins, each juror instinctively starts to construct her own mental "trial story" because the story format is the easiest and most familiar way to organize and remember new information. Story actually serves as a mnemonic device that helps jurors make sense of the evidence quickly and efficiently.[45]

The jurors' individual trial stories serve as a sort of metaphorical "glue" that holds the disparate facts of our case together. Put another way, the power

---

42. *Id.*
43. The concept of "priming" explains why people respond more quickly and accurately to prior stimuli, even though they cannot consciously recall the stimuli. E.T. Higgins et al, *Category Accessibility & Impression Formation,* 13 J. Exper. Soc. Psychol. 141–54 (1977); Nira Liberman et al, *Completed vs. Interrupted Priming: Reduced Accessibility from Post-Fulfillment Inhibition,* 43 J. Exper. Soc. Psychol. 258–64 (2007).
44. Willa Cather, O Pioneers! (1913) Part II, Ch. 4.
45. Nancy Pennington & Reid Hastie, *The Story Model for Juror Decision-Making, in* Inside the Juror: The Psychology of Juror Decision-Making 192–221 (1993).

of story provides a conceptual framework or "schema" that lends cohesiveness to disjointed bits and pieces of evidence.

Juror trial stories are disproportionately influenced by what they hear first ("the primacy effect"). This initial "trial story construct" shapes and colors the jurors' perceptions of our entire case because it serves as the filter through which they process the remainder of the evidence.[46]

Once formed, these trial stories are highly resistant to change because jurors do not revisit and revise their trial stories in response to newly introduced evidence.[47] As a result, once jurors have taken an initial position, they quickly become entrenched in it. Thereafter, they spend the rest of the trial *selectively* listening to the evidence, searching for facts that support and justify their initial position because they don't want to change it—even in the face of compelling evidence to the contrary.[48]

If we're representing the plaintiff, this is a huge advantage since we present evidence first. If the story we tell is sufficiently compelling, jurors are likely to adopt it as their own. Our trial story then becomes the lens through which jurors view all the rest of the evidence.

Primacy and recency ought to affect our trial strategy because how we order our proof determines what jurors will focus on. As plaintiff's counsel, we want them to focus on the opposing party's wrongdoing. Therefore, we should begin our opening statement by focusing on the target defendant(s) and describing each of his wrongful acts. (This should not be used as an opportunity to attack the defendant personally, but merely to attack his conduct.) Our goal is to put the target defendant in the jury's mind immediately. Only *after* we've described his wrongdoing should we address the actions of our client.

3. Primacy, Cognitive Dissonance, and Sunk Costs

Whenever our thoughts, beliefs, attitudes, and/or actions are inconsistent with one another, we experience psychological discomfort or **cognitive dissonance**.[49] Basic instinct compels us to minimize or eliminate cognitive

---

46.   Solomon E. Asch, *Forming Impressions of Personality,* 41 J. ABNORMAL & SOC. PSYCHOL. 258–90 (1947).
47.   Loren J. Chapman & Jean Chapman, *Illusory Correlations as an Obstacle to the Use of Valid Psychodiagnostic Tests,* 74 J. ABNORMAL PSYCHOL. 271–80 (1969); Mark Snyder, *When Belief Creates Reality, in* 18 ADVANCES IN EXPERIMENTAL SOC. PSYCHOL. 247–305 (L. Berkowitz, ed.1984).
48.   Asher Konat et al, *Reasons for Confidence,* 6 J. EXPER. PSYCHOL.: HUMAN LEARNING & MEMORY 107–18 (1980); Derek Koehler, *Explanation, Imagination, and Confidence in Judgment,* 110 PSYCHOL. BULL. 499–519 (1991); Charles G. Lord et al, *Biased Assimilation and Attitude Polarization: The Effects of Prior Theories on Subsequently Considered Evidence,* 37 J. PERSONALITY & SOC. PSYCHOL. 2098 (1979).
49.   LEON FESTINGER, A THEORY OF COGNITIVE DISSONANCE (1957).

dissonance as quickly as possible, even though we're not consciously aware of this phenomenon.[50] This tendency is even more pronounced whenever the decision regards an issue that's important to us.

This psychological phenomenon makes it difficult for us to hold two opposing viewpoints in our minds simultaneously. We instinctively want to be for something or against it because keeping an open mind merely increases the likelihood that we'll experience cognitive dissonance. This may lead us to expedite decision-making, simply because we feel better once we've made a decision. In fact, we tend to perceive neutrality as the equivalent of indecision.

At trial, the innate fear of cognitive dissonance may cause jurors to evaluate the evidence too quickly. Withholding judgment and keeping an open mind until they have all the facts is counter-intuitive for many jurors, particularly if the decision we're asking them to make has personal importance for them.

The principle of **sunk costs** also plays a part in premature decision-making. Whenever we make a decision, we feel personally invested in it. We prefer to move forward rather than look back, because reconsidering decisions already made only increases our level of cognitive dissonance.[51] Continuing to invest cognitive resources in an endeavor despite diminishing returns appears to be a waste of time and mental effort, which is dissonant with our inherent belief that we're logical and reasonable people. Therefore, the more "cognitive capital" we have invested in a decision, the less likely we are to question it.[52]

Examples of sunk costs abound. We refuse to get rid of expensive shoes we never wear because they cost too much to merely cast aside. Our government probably stayed too long in Vietnam because too many lives were lost and too much money spent. Rather than alter or change a prior decision to make better decisions in the future, we stubbornly stay the course because we instinctively fear that changing course may create additional cognitive dissonance. This is why jurors are reluctant to look back and question decisions they've already made. This reluctance merely increases as the trial progresses; therefore, our best opportunity to persuade jurors is at the beginning of trial, when their perceptions of the evidence are more malleable.

---

50. John M. Neale & Martin Katahn, *Anxiety, Choice, and Stimulus,* 36 J. Personality 235–45 (1968); Alan Monat et al., *Anticipatory Stress and Coping Reactions under Various Conditions of Uncertainty,* J. Personality & Soc. Psychol. 237 (1972).
51. Hal Arkes & Catherine Blumer, *The Psychology of Sunk Cost,* 35 Organ. Behav. & Human Decision Processes, 124–40 (1985).
52. *Id.*

4. The Recency Effect

A similar phenomenon is the **recency effect**.[53] If our spouse calls us at work and asks us to run a few errands on the way home, we're likely to remember not only the first errand but the last as well—simply because we haven't had time to forget it yet. We can still retrieve the information for the brief time that it remains in working or short-term memory; however, the recency effect dissipates more quickly than the primacy effect. Consequently, as time passes, we're more likely to remember the first errand rather than the last.[54]

If a trial is lengthy, the recency effect becomes more prominent. All else being equal, this tends to favor the defense.[55] We can capitalize on the recency effect by using foreshadowing. For example, we can conclude our direct examination of a witness by saying, "I'd like to ask you just a few more questions." Similarly, in closing argument, we can end by saying, "Before I sit down, I want to remind you . . . ." Signaling that the end is near encourages jurors to pay closer attention to what you say. It's also important to conclude each day with something memorable for jurors to ponder overnight, which primes them for the next day of trial.

B. Repetition, Rehearsal, and Chunking

Repetition and rehearsal (practicing what we've learned) enhance memory. That's how we learned early childhood lessons: we repeated new information by rehearsing it over and over until we knew it. What we probably failed to realize is that we learned the information in "chunks."

Chunking is a mnemonic device that enhances memory.[56] Whenever we chunk units of information such as words, letters, numbers, or information, into discrete groups of four to seven, we remember them more easily. Seven items may be the maximum amount of information we can easily remember, plus or minus two.[57] This explains why telephone numbers were initially seven digits. Even now, we use chunking to remember ten-digit telephone numbers by dividing them into three separate chunks: the three-digit area code, the first three digits, and finally, the last four digits.

---

53. Atkinson & Shiffrin, *supra* note 38.
54. Miller & Campbell, *supra* note 41.
55. *Id.* There are, however, a variety of variables at play here, depending on whether the two presentations are pro or con, separated by more or less than a week, etc. Therefore, it's difficult to do little more than make broad generalizations about the primacy and recency effects.
56. George Miller, *The Magical Number Seven, Plus or Minus Two: Some Limits on Our Capacity to Process Information,* 63 PSYCHOL. REV. 81–97 (1956). Miller's studies on memory consistently showed that test subjects could hold roughly five to nine items in short-term memory, the average being seven.
57. *Id.*

More recent research suggests that our "pure" short-term memory capacity has a limit of only about four items, plus or minus one.[58] Short-term memory limits can vary, however, depending on the material to be recalled. The more complex the material, the fewer items we're likely to retain.

When we were young, our elementary school teachers trained us to recite the alphabet in chunks. We repeated our letters in a sing-song voice in groups of up to seven letters at a time, which helped us encode the alphabet in memory. (Singing also enhances memory, although it's rarely effective in the courtroom.[59]) Our teachers knew that repetition, chunking, and rehearsal could enhance our ability to remember what we had learned. They also knew that displaying the alphabet on classroom walls and making us write our letters down on paper would help encode them into both visual and acoustic memory. This is how we transferred the letters of the alphabet from short-term into long-term memory, thereby preventing the decay of important concepts we needed to learn.

As lawyers, we must remember that we, too, are teachers. We must teach jurors about our case in a meaningful, memorable way by simplifying difficult information and breaking it into chunks. This not only alleviates the problem of "information overload," it also addresses the problem of **decision avoidance**, which occurs whenever we ask jurors to remember too much information too quickly.[60]

When decision-making becomes too difficult, jurors are likely to respond in one of two ways: (1) they may stop paying attention and refuse to make a decision (decision avoidance); or (2) they may make hasty decisions without careful deliberation or reflection and leap to improper conclusions.[61] We can discourage this by chunking our evidence into discrete, easily recognizable segments that help jurors absorb critical pieces of evidence without feeling overwhelmed.

We should organize our witness examinations into chunks. On direct examination, for example, it's helpful to begin each series of related questions

---

58. For a detailed discussion of the evidence, *see* Nelson Cowan, *The Magical Number 4 in Short-Term Memory: A Reconsideration of Mental Storage Capacity,* 24 BEHAVIORAL & BRAIN SCI. 87–185 (2000). *See* pages 116–19 for an effort to reconcile Miller's classic study with Cowan's newer theory.

59. Ellen K. Carruth, *The Effects of Singing and the Spaced Retrieval Technique on Improving Face-Name Recognition in Nursing Home Residents with Memory Loss,* 34(3) J. OF MUSIC THERAPY 165–86 (Fall 1997).

60. Richard E. Petty & Blair G. Jarvis, *An Individual Difference Perspective on Assessing Cognitive Processes, in* ANSWERING QUESTIONS: METHODOLOGY FOR DETERMINING COGNITIVE AND COMMUNICATIVE PROCESSES IN SURVEY RESEARCH, 221–57 (Norbert Schwarz & Seymour Sudman, eds. 1996).

61. *Id. See also* Donna M. Webster & W. Kruglanski Arie, *Individual Differences in Need for Cognitive Closure,* 67 J. PERSONALITY & SOC. PSYCHOL. 1049–62 (1994).

with a "headline" that clearly identifies the topic for discussion. Cueing the witness helps her stay on topic, allows her to formulate more precise answers, and suggests an appropriate pace for relaying information: "Tell the jury where you were on the night of July twelfth at seven o'clock." This "headline" not only improves the witness's testimony: it also puts what she's saying into proper context for the jurors, which enhances memory.

Cross-examination should usually be organized in *topical* chunks of information so jurors don't get lost and miss the point:

> Let's talk about your claim of self-defense. You hit Mr. Smith first, didn't you? His nose started to bleed? It was actually broken, wasn't it? And it was only after you broke his nose that he struck back at you? And when he did, you pulled a knife on him?"

After exhausting that topic, we can move to another in the same fashion:

> Let's take a look at that knife with the jury. This is no pocket knife, is it? It's not something you use at work? It has a six-inch blade?

And so on.

Similarly, we should chunk our openings and closings into digestible, bite-sized pieces. This not only enhances juror retention: it helps us as well. It's much easier to remember an opening or closing as four separate five-minute chunks of information rather than one twenty-minute chunk.

We have long recognized the importance of **the rhetorical "triad."** Chunking words, phrases, and other discrete pieces of information into groups of three has a particularly lyrical quality in the English language, which inspires jurors to pay attention. But we should acknowledge that three is not a *maximum* number since research clearly demonstrates that jurors have a much greater capacity for retention—four to seven items at a time, depending on the complexity of the information to be remembered.[62]

C. "Digesting" and "Linking" the Evidence

Because jurors must absorb large amounts of new and often contradictory evidence during trial, they need to have a chance to mentally **digest** each chunk of new information as it is presented to transfer it from short-term to long-term memory before they forget it. If they're able to **link** newly presented evidence to older information already stored in memory, they'll remember it better and for a longer period of time.

---

62. *See* Cowan, *supra* note 58.

Linking (also referred to as **associative memory**) enhances our ability to remember one concept or idea by connecting it to others already stored in memory.[63] Facts learned in isolation are likely to be forgotten or displaced by newer information; but if we're able to link several related facts together, we actually create neural networks or patterns in our brain that facilitate learning and retention. Helping jurors understand how one discrete fact relates to and builds on another creates a link that enhances their memory of the evidence by facilitating transfer of these related facts from short-term to long-term memory.

If our case involves complex information that jurors cannot comprehend on their own, we should hire an expert witness who can help jurors relate the evidence to their own life experiences. Encouraging our experts to use exhibits and real-life analogies will help jurors create neural associations or "links" that enable them to understand things that might otherwise be too difficult or esoteric for them to comprehend with ease.

D. Using Multiple Sensory Channels

Jurors constantly encode information during trial. We can help them encode critical portions of the evidence more accurately by using visual aids and exhibits, which invite jurors to encode information both visually and acoustically. Using more than one method of encoding significantly enhances their memory of the evidence.

Our visuals don't have to be fancy or expensive, merely effective. For example, we could do something as simple as draw a line down the middle of a chalkboard and label one side, "What Plaintiff Did" and the other side, "What Defendant Did." This allows us to compare and contrast the behavior of our client with that of the opposing party both aurally and visually. When using simple exhibits such as this, we should put the major points we want to emphasize on the right side of the board since jurors read from left to right; therefore, their eyes will naturally come to rest on the right side of any writing.

We can graphically illustrate the parties' respective decisions by creating a simple decision tree. This is particularly effective if the opposing party made a series of bad decisions that ultimately harmed our client. We can illustrate all of the options that were available to the opposing party and clearly show that he disregarded other clearly superior options—options that would not have resulted in harm to our client. Nevertheless, he consistently made the worst possible choice in each instance.

---

63. Eliot R. Smith & Sarah Queller, *Mental Representations, in* SOC. COGNITION, 5–27 (Marilyn Brewer et al, eds., 2004).

All of us remember information best when we can tie it to a particular *person or place* in memory.[64] For example, if we show jurors a picture or video of the place where an important, transformative event in the case occurred, we can help them link the event to that place. This helps them reconstruct the event more accurately when they later try to recall what happened. This allows us to position our "evidentiary camera" at the places where we want jurors to make "mental movies" of what happened. This not only enhances their memory of the underlying event: it also ensures that every juror will have the same mental picture of what actually happened.

For example, if we discuss the intersection where an auto accident occurred, each juror may have a different mental image of that intersection. This may lead jurors to disagree about what actually happened during deliberations. But if we introduce a picture or diagram of the intersection and show the respective positions of the vehicles involved, each one of the jurors will have the same mental image in their minds. This prevents one juror's inaccurate memory from contaminating the more accurate memories of less vocal jurors who may be reluctant to disagree with him.

We should create visuals for each key element of our case. Tying words and images together not only enhances juror memory, it enhances our presentation skills. If we organize our presentation to correspond with the visuals we intend to use at trial, it can dramatically improve our ability to clarify what we're going to say next without relying on notes. Our presentation will also look more polished if our exhibits seem to track exactly what we're saying.

In some cases, sound may be an essential element. For example, presume our clients live in the flight path of an airport that has just expanded its runways to accommodate a large Federal Express hub. The noise of low-flying jet engines has essentially rendered their home unlivable. If we sue the airport authority for creating a nuisance, the best possible evidence will be a sound recording of a huge jet coming in for a landing recorded from the back porch of our client's home. Playing this at trial so jurors can hear the noise for themselves will probably be the most persuasive evidence in the case.

E. Creating a Memorable Trial Story

All of us organize information into stories because it's the easiest, most natural way to remember it. We remember events as stories and relate them to other people in story format. But there's an art to effective storytelling.

Although the facts of a case may seem straightforward at first, there are multiple ways to tell our client's story. We must find the *best* way to tell it by

---

64. William F. Brewer & James C. Trevens, *Role of Schemata in Memory for Places,* 13(2) Cognitive Psychol. 207–30 (Apr. 1981).

predicting how jurors are likely to sort out the competing narratives at trial. If we take the elemental facts of our case and translate them into the universal language of human experience, we can create a trial story that jurors are likely to remember and adopt as their own. If *our* trial story becomes *their* trial story, we're more likely to win the case.

1. Not Telling Too Much

"The secret of being a bore is to tell everything."
Voltaire[65]

The story we tell in opening statement must be minimalist. We want our opening to serve as little more than a suggested outline or schema for jurors to use in fashioning their own personal trial stories. The more easily they can incorporate the essential elements of our trial story into their own, the more likely they are to adopt our version of events as true.

It's easy to err on the side of presenting too much information because we're afraid of leaving an important fact untold. Although we might think that this approach minimizes risk, it merely dilutes our message, breeds confusion, and gives jurors more information to disagree with.

We win cases by picking the right facts to tell—without arguing, embellishing, or interpreting them. All good stories should be a voyage of discovery for the reader or listener. If we tell just enough of our story to put the evidence in proper context, we can pique the jurors' curiosity and leave them wanting to know more.

2. Making Our Trial Story Memorable and "Available"

We begin creating our trial story by asking ourselves the following questions: Which elements of my client's story will resonate with the jury? Where should my story begin? Who should tell it? From what point of view? (Generally, the best point of view is that of the person who suffered the greatest loss.) What tools (e.g., PowerPoint presentations, exhibits, visual aids, etc.) should I use to make the story come alive?

To take advantage of primacy and the stress of indecision, we should begin our opening statement by making evidence of our opponent's wrongdoing immediately "available" to the jury. (See discussion of the **availability heuristic** in chapter seven.) If we talk about our client before mentioning the opposing party (or parties) and his improper behavior, we've merely encouraged jurors to scrutinize and judge her behavior more harshly than his.

---

65. Voltaire, Sixth Discourse on the Nature of Man (1738).

We must tell our trial story in words that are familiar to jurors. Speaking their language enhances the likelihood that they will believe what we say. If we can find particular words and phrases that will resonate with them (which can be discovered in focus groups), jurors will be more likely to remember these "sound bites" and repeat them to their fellow jurors during deliberations.

3. Offering Multiple Points of Reentry

The jurors' level of attention will inevitably wax and wane during trial. It's almost as if their minds are programmed to take periodic "commercial breaks" to avoid information overload. This process is analogous to "channel surfing" while watching television. If we find a show that briefly captures our interest, we may lose interest in it and change channels. If we can't find something more interesting to watch, we'll turn back to the first show and stick with it—*if* we're able to figure out what happened in the interim. Our trial story must allow jurors to do the same thing.

Every good story offers multiple points of reentry because it's constructed in a way that allows us to piece together the parts we've missed while thinking about other things. If our trial story is consistent, compelling, and tightly drawn, jurors will be able to pick up the thread of it easily, even after periods of inattention. If they cannot effectively rejoin the evidence in progress, however, they're likely to remain inattentive.

F. Using Memorable Themes

A theme is the larger-than-life moral foundation on which our evidence rests, much like a parable or an Aesop's fable. A good theme places our client's story squarely into the universal human story by making it seem larger and more important than the facts alone. Compelling themes are powerful psychological unifiers that tie all of the evidence together in a way that is memorable and meaningful for each of the jurors, even those who may be predisposed against us.

Great themes tap into the jurors' broader sense of right and wrong, not merely the specifics of what's right and wrong in our particular case. Jurors will be more willing to act if they believe their verdict will have far-reaching consequences that extend beyond the individual litigants and the case facts. If we can awaken the jury's sense of moral outrage by framing the case as a clear choice between right and wrong, the jurors themselves will feel that they've been personally wronged by what happened—*if* our theme is consistent with their personal notions of right and wrong.

Because universal truths transcend precise definition, there will always be multiple ways to articulate our themes. We dare not take the risk of having only one theme or defining it in only one particular way because no single word or phrase should be expected to carry that burden on its own. Each juror absorbs and interprets the evidence differently, so if our specific articulation of a theme either offends or fails to resonate with some of the jurors, we've done more harm than good.

Although we want our themes to be short, pithy, and easy for jurors to understand, remember, and repeat in the jury room, they must be more than mere "impact statements." An impact statement is simply an attention-getting slogan or clever turn of phrase—for example, "The defendant company was too busy talking care of business to be careful." This is but one expression of the larger, underlying theme of corporate greed and indifference. When overused, impact statements appear to be little more than pandering or cheap advertising.

Attorney Mark Mandell of Providence, Rhode Island, is fond of saying, "A good theme reveals meaning without committing the error of over-defining it." For example, in the O. J. Simpson criminal trial, much credit has been given to Johnny Cochran's one-line impact statement, "If it doesn't fit, you must acquit." This catchphrase was not Cochran's theme: it was merely a powerful refrain that made his larger theme of "wrongful accusation" more memorable. Everyone has been wrongly accused at one time or another, so this was the real theme that resonated with the jury.

G. Using Fables, Parables, Allegories, and Myths

Fables, parables, allegories, and myths make particularly compelling themes because they tell stories that speak in generalities and universal truths rather than abstractions. Jurors find it easier to relate to a morality tale than a legal abstraction such as "justice," "reasonable doubt," or "negligence." Consider the following example:

> A man walks down to a river bank and sees masses of dead bodies floating downstream. Being a good man, he starts pulling these dead bodies out of the river, one at a time. He throws each body over his shoulder, carries it up the river bank, and buries it. He does this until he's completely exhausted and thoroughly depressed. Finally, he says to himself, "I just can't do this anymore."
>
> So he walks a little further up the river and sees people who are dying in the river. Being a good man, he jumps into the river

and starts pulling out the dying people, one at a time. He drags them to the river bank and resuscitates them; but soon, he's exhausted yet again.

So he walks a little further up the river and sees one man throwing people into the river. The moral of the story is that if you catch the problem at the source, you can cure it once and for all.[66]

This story could be effective in a products liability case or any other case in which the defendant should have taken preventive measures but didn't, and someone was injured as a result. It animates our client's story and universalizes it by linking what happened to her to a simple story that jurors can relate to. This is how the power of story and theme can work in tandem to lend context and meaning to our closing argument.

---

66.   This so-called "River Parable" is attributed to many people, primarily Saul Alinsky.

CHAPTER FOUR

WHY AND HOW JURORS MANIPULATE PERCEPTION AND MEMORY

I. Introduction

This chapter begins our discussion of *why and how* jurors instinctively alter their perceptions and memories to comport with what they presently believe or want to believe. We also discuss why and how this affects their decisions at trial. The rest of the book is devoted to various aspects of these topics.

A. Basic Instinct: Maslow's Hierarchical Pyramid

Abraham Maslow was an American psychologist who theorized that all human beings have a clear hierarchy of needs. He described these primal needs in order of importance in his famous "pyramid of needs," now widely known as **Maslow's Hierarchical Pyramid.**[1]

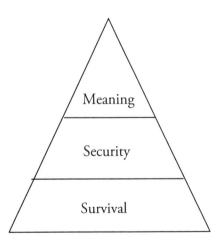

---

1. Abraham H. Maslow, *A Theory of Human Motivation,* 50 PSYCHOL. REV. 370 (1943). There has been some controversy as to whether there is a "definite" hierarchy of needs; however, the theory is generally well-regarded and influential. For a revised view of the pyramid from an evolutionary psychological perspective, *see* Douglass T. Kenrick et al, *Renovating the Pyramid of Needs: Contemporary Extensions Built Upon Ancient Foundations,* 5 PERSPECTIVES ON PSYCHOL. SCI. 1–74 (2010).

The most important human needs are those necessary to survival such as water, food, and sleep. These basic physiological needs form the base of Maslow's Pyramid and must be met before all others. Once these needs are satisfied, we can advance to the next level of the pyramid, which encompasses our need for safety and security. Thereafter, we move to a sense of belonging, self-esteem, purpose, and ultimately, meaning.[2]

B. The Primal Need for Self-Preservation and Protection

The primal needs at the base of Maslow's pyramid (which are loosely referred to as "basic or primal instincts") are the most powerful human motivators. These essential needs automatically (unconsciously) drive many of the decisions we make in life because they literally keep us alive and well.

Although most of us are able to meet our basic needs for food, clothing, and shelter, our need for protection is more problematic. We know it's not easy to keep ourselves safe in a dangerous and unpredictable world. This is why the random occurrence of adverse events frightens us: it forces us to confront the harsh reality that we can't always protect ourselves from harm.

The mere thought of being unable to protect ourselves is intolerable because fear is a powerful primal emotion that evokes a disproportionately strong response.[3] Whenever a primitive portion of our brain (the **amygdala**[4]) perceives a threat to our safety or well-being, we instinctively react by trying to eliminate it.

If the perceived threat is sufficiently grave, we can have a variety of responses including, but not limited to, one of three things: (1) we stand and fight; (2) we run away; or (3) we mentally alter our perception of the threat, whether real or imagined, to make it seem less frightening. The first two options are our basic "fight or flight" response in action. The third option, known as **reappraisal** (which simply means to change how we think about a threat or stressor[5]) is one we're less familiar with, but it wields considerable influence over our thoughts and behavior.

Whenever we feel threatened, we not only seek to eliminate the threat: we also feel compelled to identify or explain its source so that we can protect ourselves from similar threats in the future. We instinctively search for some-

---

2. *Id.*

3. Paul Ekman, *Basic Emotions, in* Handbook of Cognition and Emotion 45–60 (Tim Dagleish & Mick Power, eds. 1999).

4. The amygdala is the part of our brain associated with fear and aggression that triggers our "fight or flight" response. It plays an important role in visual learning and memory. Simon Killcross et al., *Different Types of Fear-Conditioned Behaviour Mediated by Separate Nuclei within Amygdala*, 388 Nature 377–80 (1997).

5. Lawrence E. Williams et al, *The Unconscious Regulation of Emotion: Nonconscious Reappraisal Goals Modulate Emotional Reactivity*, 9 Emotions 847–54 (2009).

one or something to blame. In other words, we "explain" adversity (or the mere threat of it) by assigning fault or blame.[6] Once we think we've identified the source of the threat, we usually feel reassured and less afraid.

If, however, we're unable to identify or explain what caused the threat or adverse event, we may consciously or unconsciously alter our perception of it. In other words, we reappraise what we think about the threat, perhaps by generating an explanation of our own—preferably one that allows us to believe that nothing similar could ever happen to us.[7] Psychologists refer to these types of self-generated explanations as **cognitive coping strategies**,[8] which involve altering how we think about a stressful situation.

C. Cognitive Coping Strategies

Cognitive coping strategies are simply mental mechanisms that satisfy our overwhelming need to feel safe and protected by helping us deal with perceived threats from actual predators or merely from "threatening" information. These coping strategies allow us to live without being constantly afraid of what might happen to us.[9] Although cognitive coping strategies alleviate stress and help preserve our sanity, they also engender predictable thinking errors.[10] The most common thinking errors are discussed in this and the chapters that follow.

1. Belief in a "Just World"

Our primal need for protection gives rise to the **belief in a just world**. This cognitive coping strategy leads us to assume that good things happen to "good" people and bad things happen to "bad" people because that's how the world ought to work. A just world should always reward good behavior and punish bad behavior (other than our own, perhaps) because justice must always prevail in the end. This belief allows us to see the world as the orderly, predictable place we so desperately want and need it to be.

We selfishly see ourselves as inherently "good" people because a positive self-concept is essential to our well-being.[11] As long as we behave properly, i.e., as long as we're "good," we don't have to worry about the consequences of being "bad."

---

6. *See* MELVIN J. LERNER, THE BELIEF IN A JUST WORLD: A FUNDAMENTAL DELUSION (1980).
7. Williams et al, *supra* note 5.
8. Susan Folkman & Judith T. Moskowitz, *Coping: Pitfalls and Promise*, 55 ANN. REV. OF PSYCHOL. 745–74 (2004).
9. *Id.*
10. JUDITH BECK, COGNITIVE THERAPY: BASICS AND BEYOND (1995).
11. Constantine Sedikides & Michael J. Strube, *Self-Evaluation: To Thine Own Self Be Good, To Thine Own Self Be Sure, To Thine Own Self Be True, and To Thine Own Self Be Better*, 29 ADVANCES IN EXPER. SOC. PSYCHOL. 209–69 (1997).

2. The Illusion of Control

Our belief in a just world gives rise to another cognitive coping strategy. Everyone knows that actions have predictable consequences; therefore, if we believe that we're able to predict potential outcomes in life with a high degree of accuracy, we can convince ourselves that we can control what happens to us. This self-protective fiction is referred to as the **illusion of control**.[12] As long as we're able to distinguish right from wrong and good from bad, we should, in theory, be able to behave in the manner that a just world demands.[13]

We desperately want (or, more accurately, *need*) to live in a world in which we are masters of our own fate. We want every problem to have an easily identifiable solution. We demand explanations for every "bad" outcome. We're uncomfortable with ambiguity and indecision because we crave order and stability in our lives. Therefore, believing we can control outcomes and protect ourselves from all real or imagined harm is far more palatable than admitting the world is a dangerous and unpredictable place where innocent people get hurt, no matter how "good," prudent, and responsible they may be.

Although we're *objectively* aware that we have limited control over what happens to us, we tend to cast rational thinking aside whenever we're afraid. We're willing to believe whatever it takes to avoid living in constant fear of what might happen to us.[14]

Unfortunately, we tend to overrate our own ability to predict and control outcomes while underestimating that of others. For example, whenever we play a game of chance like tossing a coin or playing the lottery, we develop the illusion of being in control. (This illusion keeps casinos in business and gamblers in debt.) If the game of chance also involves skill, we're even more likely to unreasonably believe that we can control the outcome.[15]

D. Cognitive Dissonance

Our belief in a just world and the illusion of control work well as long as the world rocks along as we think it should. But these beliefs are challenged whenever something "bad" inexplicably happens to a "good" person. For example, if we learn about a frightening, unpredictable event in which some-

---

12. Ellen J. Langer, *The Illusion of Control*, 32 J. PERSONALITY & SOC. PSYCHOL. 311 (1975).
13. Tom Pyszczynski et al, *Why Do People Need Self-Esteem? A Theoretical and Empirical Review*, 130 PSYCHOL. BULL. 435–68 (2004).
14. LERNER, *supra* note 6.
15. Ellen J. Langer & Jane Roth, *Heads I Win, Tails It's Chance: The Illusion of Control as a Function of the Sequence of Outcomes in a Purely Chance Task*, 32 J. PERSONALITY & SOC. PSYCHOL. 951 (1975).

one was seriously injured or killed through no fault of her own, we can't help but wonder: "What if that had happened to me? How would I have reacted?"

We feel personally threatened by these sorts of bad outcomes because we're unable to reconcile what happened with our notion of a just world and the illusion of control. This causes us to experience **cognitive dissonance**, or psychological discomfort, because we're unable to resolve this inconsistency with our deeply held attitudes and beliefs.[16]

The anxiety of cognitive dissonance compels us to seek an explanation for what happened: one that will allow us to reconcile the adverse event with our belief in a just world. This often leads us to make unfounded assumptions in order to square what *actually* happened with what we believe *should* have happened in a just world.

Interestingly, we often choose to eliminate life's ambiguities and injustices by convincing ourselves they simply don't exist. This can obviously affect our ability to make wise and rational decisions.

II. Searching for Explanations in the Courtroom

The self-protective fictions of a just world and the illusion of control are often challenged in the courtroom. When this happens, jurors may resort to Levels I and II decision-making. These types of lower level decisions may surprise and confound us.

In a criminal case, for example, jurors may find it difficult to accept that a seemingly "good" person could be the victim of a serious crime. But if the defendant appears to be a "bad" person or if he intentionally did a "bad" thing, jurors will find it easier to render a guilty verdict because a just world demands punishment for such people. (Unfortunately, the fact that someone is merely charged with a criminal offense can make them seem "bad" in the eyes of some jurors.)

Whenever jurors are confronted with evidence that a seemingly "good" defendant has committed a serious crime, they experience cognitive dissonance. Since "good" people don't do "bad" things in their imaginary just world, jurors find it difficult to reconcile this belief with the facts of the case. (This tendency is actually **defensive attribution**, which is discussed in chapter six. The belief in a just world and the illusion of control are the underlying causes of defensive attribution.)

---

16. Leon Festinger, A Theory of Cognitive Dissonance (1957).

A. How Jurors Manipulate Their Perceptions in Criminal Cases

If we represent a criminal defendant the jurors are likely to perceive as a "good" person, we have a distinct advantage at trial. Not only does the criminal burden of proof work in our favor, jurors may also refuse to believe that our "good" client behaved "badly" enough to merit conviction.

Many commentators believe cognitive coping strategies played a role in the surprising acquittals of William Kennedy Smith and O. J. Simpson. Both defendants were young, attractive, wealthy, and famous. (*See* chapter six on the ***attractiveness bias***.) Both were charged with serious crimes, yet both were acquitted, despite arguably strong evidence of guilt. Why?

The fact that innocent young women could be raped or murdered by seemingly "good" men is incongruous with the notion of a just world and the illusion of control. If attractive men who appear to "good" people can commit such awful crimes, how can jurors—particularly female jurors—ever be safe from sexual predators if they're unable to identify and avoid these "bad" men?

In cases where juror perceptions of the defendant are at odds with the prosecution's evidence, jurors may resort to cognitive coping strategies to alleviate cognitive dissonance. In fact, a sampling of comments made by jurors shortly after they acquitted William Kennedy Smith of rape suggests how they justified their verdict:

> "I just find it hard to believe that someone with that much money would have to resort to rape to get what he wants."[17]

> "He probably just got carried away. Pretty girl. You know. That's how guys are. I have sons myself."[18]

> "I thought I made a good decision, and everyone else seems to think so, too."[19]

> "[H]e wouldn't need to rape anyone."[20]

Jurors obviously found it hard to imagine the handsome young Dr. Smith as a sexual predator because he didn't appear threatening to *them*.

Whenever jurors sense a threat to their own safety or well-being, whether real or imagined, they're often motivated to respond in one of two ways: (1) they may simply disregard the threatening evidence; or (2) they may alter

---

17. Mary I. Christine Evans, *Courtyard 'Jury' Has Own View on Trial*, MIAMI HERALD, Dec. 3, 1991.

18. *Id.*

19. Nancy S. Marder, *Deliberations and Disclosures: A Study of Post-Verdict Interviews of Jurors* 82 IOWA L. REV. 465 (1997).

20. Mary I. Coombs, *Telling the Victim's Story*, 2 TEX. J. WOMEN L. 277, 301 (1993.

their perceptions of the evidence to make it more consistent with what they believe or want to believe is true.[21] These automatic responses are examples of cognitive coping strategies that help jurors eliminate the conflict between reality and their cherished belief in a just world and the need for protection.

Because such decisions are made on the lowest levels of our hierarchy of decision-making, jurors are generally unaware of their reliance on cognitive coping strategies. We, however, must be keenly aware of how these strategies operate because they can dramatically affect juror perceptions of our case.

B. How Jurors Manipulate Their Perceptions in Civil Cases

It is inherently difficult to represent an injured plaintiff because no one wants to be a plaintiff. No one even wants to *imagine* being a plaintiff, particularly in a case that involves serious injury illness, death, or a condition or loss that could potentially affect us personally, such as the loss of a child.

When jurors are confronted with a seemingly "good" plaintiff who was seriously injured through no fault of her own, they begin to experience cognitive dissonance. This, in turn, activates their primal "fight or flight" response, which causes them to react as if there were a real and personal threat to their *own* safety.

As jurors automatically "flee" from the thought of what happened to the plaintiff, logic and reason often go with them. The line between fact and fantasy begins to blur as jurors try to convince themselves that nothing similar could ever happen to them. They don't want to acknowledge that bad things actually do happen to good people—*particularly when no intent to harm is present.*

The illusion of control also makes jurors reluctant to admit there was nothing the plaintiff could have done to prevent the harm. They begin to wonder how the plaintiff could have "allowed" such a bad thing to happen, which presupposes she had the ability to control the outcome. This automatic response stems from the jurors' desperate need to believe they're masters of their own fate and can control what happens to them.

Although jurors don't enjoy confronting the unpleasant reality of what happened, they feel compelled to explain the bad outcome because a "just world" demands accountability.[22] Assigning blame also helps alleviate their cognitive dissonance.

---

21.   Charles G. Lord, *Biased Assimilation and Attitude Polarization: The Effects of Prior Theories on Subsequently Considered Evidence*, 37 J. PERSONALITY & SOC. PSYCHOL. 2098–2109 (1979).
22.   LERNER, *supra* note 6.

As they search for explanations, jurors consider all the things *they* would have done differently had they been in the plaintiff's position. This is how they convince themselves that they, unlike the plaintiff, could have controlled the situation and avoided injury—even if the facts objectively show the situation was beyond her control. This tendency obviously inures to the benefit of the defense. (*See also* the discussion of **counterfactual thinking** and chapter six on the **fundamental attribution error**. All of these concepts are inextricably interrelated.)

Although jurors themselves are completely unaware of it, their automatic reaction to the plaintiff's predicament tends to be disproportionately strong and inappropriate to the situation because it's based in fear.[23] *The jurors' overwhelming need to protect themselves from all real or imagined harm may prove stronger than their need to accurately and objectively assign blame.*

The simplest and most satisfying explanation is often to blame the plaintiff herself since the defendant had no intent to harm her. This is an easy way for jurors to reconcile what happened with what they so desperately need to believe, even if there's no evidence of contributory negligence. Alternatively, jurors may presume the plaintiff must be a "bad" person who got exactly what she deserved.[24] (See discussions on social and cultural biases in chapters seven and eight.) Why else would a just world permit this to happen?

Jurors tend to unconsciously allay their fears of suffering similar outcomes by altering the case facts in a way that makes them feel less vulnerable and more in control. Although their self-generated "explanations" help jurors feel safe once again, these explanations may be objectively irrational and totally unsupported by the evidence. We need to be prepared to deal with these cognitive coping strategies, particularly if we're representing the plaintiff.

C. How Plaintiff's Counsel Can Respond

Whenever jurors may be inclined to hold the injured plaintiff to an unreasonable or impossible standard of care, we must act to prevent this from happening. Otherwise, our client will have to live with the unintended consequences of their decision.

Cognitive dissonance makes jurors eager to allocate fault. They don't enjoy the stress of indecision, so they're quick—often too quick—to decide what happened and whose fault it was. We can help jurors eliminate the stress of indecision and counteract their natural inclination to blame our client for

---

23. Lerner, *supra* note 6.
24. For a detailed discussion of who is likely to "blame the victim" and why, *see* Kees van den Bos & Marjolein Maas, *On the Psychology of the Belief in a Just World: Explaining Experimental and Rationalistic Paths to Victim-Blaming*, 35 J. Personality & Soc. Psychol. Bull. 1567–78 (2009).

what happened by immediately blaming the opposing party for what happened.

Jurors, like everyone else, tend to criticize that which they know the most about. (*See* chapter eight on the availability bias.) Therefore, what we choose to focus on usually dictates how the case will be decided.

If we begin the trial by focusing on our client (as we've often done in the past), jurors are inclined to criticize her conduct. But if we do the reverse and initially focus on the defendant, jurors will instinctively try to find fault with him instead of our client. *We need the trial to be about the opposing party and what he could have or should have done but failed to do, not about our client and what she did or didn't do.* And if there is more than one defendant, we should discuss the key defendant first, the other defendant(s) next, and the plaintiff last.

There will always be gaps in our evidence: information we haven't yet found that jurors will be looking for at trial. We need to identify these gaps before trial, and preferably before filing suit, by conducting focus groups and/or mock trials. These are the best tools for discovering critical holes in our evidence that we haven't yet identified. What focus group participants want to know tells us what jurors will need to hear at trial, which will inevitably be facts and arguments that reflect their relevant beliefs, values, and life experiences.

Once we know what to look for, we can purposefully develop evidence that will satisfy our jurors, decrease the likelihood they will blame our client for what happened, and increase the odds of winning our case. If we're unable to find critical missing facts, we should consider settling the case rather than going to trial. Leaving gaps in the evidence always favors the defendant, who has no burden of proof.

D. An Example

Presume that we represent a plaintiff who was driving to work in a terrible thunderstorm. As her car passed underneath a huge hundred-year-old tree that stood in front of an apartment building, a 200-pound tree limb fell directly onto her car, rendering her a quadriplegic. The city where the incident occurred had a tree ordinance that prohibited cutting down trees within city limits without first securing a permit.

Four years before the accident, the owner of the apartment building had tried to secure a permit from the city to remove the tree. The tree had already shed several sizeable limbs and was showing signs of rot and insect infestation. Despite this, when the city's chief arborist came out to inspect the tree, he declared that the tree posed no immediate hazard. He also noted the tree was a historic landmark that should be preserved.

The city arborist flatly refused to issue a permit to the property owner to cut the tree. The property owner didn't pursue the permitting process any further, thinking it would be futile to do so. Consequently, the tree remained in place until after the plaintiff was injured.

As counsel for the plaintiff, we may be tempted to begin our trial story by talking about the accident and how badly our client was injured. But if we do, jurors will instinctively want to distance themselves from what happened to her.

Jurors are already aware of the plaintiff's injury. If our trial story begins with the thunderstorm and the falling limb, jurors are more likely to either (1) blame the plaintiff for driving in such bad weather, or (2) attribute what happened to an act of God since no one can be held accountable for the weather. If, however, we begin our story a year before the accident—when the city denied the apartment owner's request for a permit to cut down the tree—the jurors' response is likely to be quite different.

One option is to begin our opening statement by focusing on the city arborist's decision to preserve the historic tree. This approach encourages jurors to focus on the arborist's conduct rather than that of his codefendant (the apartment owner) or the plaintiff. By simply changing the order of the underlying events, we can encourage jurors to **reappraise** or change how they think about those events.

Shifting our initial focus to the city arborist makes our case primarily about a city that takes better care of its trees than its people; secondarily about an apartment owner who fails to protect his tenants; and least of all, about our client's decision to drive during a thunderstorm. By showing the city arborist's decision not only predated, but precipitated the plaintiff's injury, we can make jurors more likely to criticize the city's conduct.

Similarly, if we begin by talking about the owner of the apartment building and his failure to maintain the tree and keep his property safe for tenants and passersby, jurors are likely to see him as primarily responsible for what happened. The decision of which defendant to blame first depends on who we want to bear the most responsibility.

If the key defendant's conduct is the focal point of our trial story, jurors feel less compelled to distance themselves from the plaintiff and her injury. Instead, they'll instinctively want to criticize the key defendant's conduct, particularly if the case facts justify framing it as intentional, unjustifiable, or extreme. Jurors are more willing to punish what they view as *exceptional* misconduct.

E. Letting Jurors Do Their Job

Jurors want to draw their own conclusions about wrongdoing. Our job is simply to provide them with clear evidence that highlights the opposing party's wrongdoing without judging it or drawing conclusions about the merits of the case. Jurors are much more willing to punish misconduct when they feel we're *inviting* them to do so by merely laying out the facts rather than demanding that they act by arguing our case. Jurors want to feel free to decide the case on their own. They certainly don't want lawyers to tell them what to do.

Remaining relatively detached and nonjudgmental enhances our credibility as an advocate. Rarely is an ad hominem attack on the opposing party merited. If we give jurors the elemental, unvarnished facts and the proper tools to do their job, they will generally arrive at the right decision.

In the next chapter, we will discuss the most common juror biases. These biases also play a significant role in altering juror perception and memory.

CHAPTER FIVE

COMMON JUROR BIASES

I. Introduction to Biases

All human beings are biased, although we don't like to think of ourselves that way. The word "bias" has a negative connotation of prejudice or bigotry in everyday usage. In social psychology, however, the term has a more neutral meaning. A **bias** is simply a preference or inclination, either positive or negative, that affects how we process information.[1] In other words, our biases are preconceived notions or opinions that predispose us to think about things in a certain way.

We form biases by repeatedly reacting to external and internal influences in a predictable, consistent manner. Some of our biases are actually primitive survival mechanisms that are grounded in self-enhancing or self-protective motives.[2] Other biases are simply an inevitable by-product of the way in which we process information.

Biases, like "heuristics" (which are discussed in chapter seven), are essentially shortcut classification schemes that help us process information more quickly and efficiently, even though they're not specifically developed for that purpose. Although the two cognitive processes operate very differently, both biases and heuristics can significantly influence our thinking and decision-making by causing us to unconsciously alter our perceptions and memories.

To more accurately gauge how jurors are likely to respond to our case, we need to understand the most common biases that jurors automatically rely on to perceive, process, and remember the evidence presented at trial. This chapter begins our discussion of **cognitive and motivational biases**, particularly those that influence juror "trial story" formulations. The next two chapters deal with **social** or **attributional biases** and **cultural biases**. Together, these biases comprise Level III of our hierarchy of decision-making. All of these biases are closely related. They also tend to operate in conjunc-

---

1. SUSAN T. FISKE & SHELLEY E. TAYLOR, SOCIAL COGNITION (2d ed. 1991).
2. Roy F. Baumeister, *The Self, in* HANDBOOK OF SOCIAL PSYCHOLOGY 680–740 (D.T. Gilbert et al, eds., 4th ed. 1998); E. Tory Higgins, *Self Knowledge Serving Self-Regulatory Functions,* 71 J. PERSONALITY & SOC. PSYCHOL. 1062–83 (1996).

tion with one another, which makes it difficult, if not impossible, to separate their application in the courtroom.

A. Linking and Neural Networking

As described in chapter two, the human brain is comprised of a complex system of neural networks that help us interpret new information by comparing or **linking** it to what we already know.[3] Because all of us are cognitive misers, we automatically conserve our cognitive resources whenever possible. As adults, one of the ways we do this is by **assimilating** new information rather than **accommodating** it. (*See* chapter two on Memory.) In other words, we try to squeeze novel concepts or ideas into existing, but ill-fitting schemata rather than create brand new schemata that would be more appropriate classifications for something we've never encountered before. We also tend to either assimilate or completely disregard new information that we disagree with—a cognitive process referred to as **biased assimilation**.

B. Biased Assimilation and Belief Perseverance

Psychological research shows that whenever we encounter new information that conflicts with what we believe or want to believe is true, we process these **counterattitudinal perceptions** in a biased manner.[4] Because our perceptions are automatically filtered through our personal belief biases, we don't necessarily believe what we see and hear; rather, we tend to see and hear what we already believe, regardless of the speaker's intent.[5]

Because biased assimilation occurs beyond our level of conscious awareness, our biases become deeply entrenched over time. Changing a bias requires enormous effort because it generates severe cognitive dissonance; therefore, we fervently cling to our biases and stubbornly refuse to change them—even *after* receiving credible, contradictory information that alters or refutes them.[6] This is why our so-called **belief biases** are said to "persevere"—because we're either unaware of or unwilling to change them.

---

3. Eliot R. Smith & Sarah Queller, *Mental Representations* in SOCIAL COGNITION 5–27 (Marilyn Brewer et al, eds.) (2004).
4. Charles G. Lord et al, *Biased Assimilation and Attitude Polarization: The Effects of Prior Theories on Subsequently Considered Evidence,* 37 J. PERSONALITY & SOCIAL PSYCHOL. 2098 (1979).
5. Edward Hut, *Do I See Only What I Expect? Evidence for an Expectancy-Guided Retrieval Model,* 58 J. PERSONALITY & SOC. PSYCHOL. 937–51 (1990).
6. Lee Ross et al., *Perseverence in Self-Perception and Social Perception: Biased Attributional Processes in the Debriefing Paradigm,* 32 J. PERSONALITY & SOC. PSCYHOL. 880–92; JUDITH BECK, COGNITIVE THERAPY: BASICS AND BEYOND (1995).

Belief perseverance is the psychological term that broadly describes how our knowledge and beliefs control the composition of our thoughts.[7] We're accustomed to relying on our own personal belief biases to make decisions in our everyday lives. We continue to cling to these belief biases because to do otherwise would create severe cognitive dissonance, which we automatically try to avoid.

Jurors do the same thing at trial. Whenever they hear evidence that conflicts with their belief biases, they often fail to evaluate it in a fair and even-handed manner by doing one of two things: (1) disregarding it entirely, or (2) changing their perceptions of the conflicting evidence to make it fit with what they presently believe.[8] Either way, jurors are more likely to disregard or distort the conflicting *evidence* rather than alter their personal belief biases. This is **biased assimilation** in action. Although biased assimilation may relieve the jurors' cognitive dissonance, it also allows them to maintain their belief biases, despite what the evidence might show.

C. Contamination of Trial Stories

Whenever we hear new "event information," we instinctively start to construct a story in our minds to interpret and make sense of what happened.[9] Psychological studies have shown that jurors do the same thing at trial—they quickly and instinctively construct a "trial story" to help them make sense of the evidence.[10] (*See* chapter two.)

Jurors begin this trial story construction process by searching for a similar "story schema" filed away in memory. They instinctively begin to compare what happened in the case to the world they know. The particular story schema they're likely to access first will be one they're accustomed to relying on in their everyday lives, largely because it's the most readily **available** in memory. It's likely to be a story that makes them think: "Oh, I've seen that happen before," "I know where this is going," or "The same thing happened to me." (*See* chapter seven on the **availability heuristic**.)

All jurors have preconceived notions about how people should behave, how events should unfold, and how things work. They use these archetypal story formulations or "prefabricated story patterns" as a frame of reference for understanding and remembering the facts of our case. This is unfortunate in two ways. First, juror story schemas will inevitably reflect the jurors'

---

7. *Id.*
8. Leon Festinger, A Theory of Cognitive Dissonance (1957).
9. Valerie F. Reyna & Charles J. Brainerd, *Fuzzy-Trace Theory: An Interim Synthesis,* 7 Learning & Individual Differences 1 (1995); Frederic Bartlett, Remembering: A Study in Experimental and Social Psychology (1932).
10. Nancy Pennington & Reid Hastie, *Evidence Evaluation in Complex Decision-Making,* 51 J. Personality & Soc. Psychol. 242–56 (1986).

personal belief biases. Second, the story schema that is *easiest* for jurors to recall won't necessarily be one that closely resembles the evidence presented at trial.

As jurors retrieve threads of these personal "story schemas" from memory, each of them automatically brings a wealth of unrelated information and experiences to bear on the evidence. This may cause jurors to unintentionally intermingle and confuse similar "story schemas" with the actual facts of the case. (*See* discussion of **contamination of memory** in chapter two.) Worse yet, jurors believe these commingled stories are true and accurate reflections of the evidence, never realizing that their perceptions and personal trial stories may be objectively incorrect. As a result, jurors may ultimately decide the case on more than its facts alone. Sadly, we never fully know the extent to which this occurs until after the verdict, if at all.

D. Linking to Juror Belief Biases

Regardless of intrinsic merit, we must deal with juror belief biases because their impact is enormous and often outcome-determinative. Since jurors themselves find it difficult to recognize and account for their own belief biases, we must do it for them.[11]

Fortunately, most biases operate in fairly systematic, consistent, and predictable patterns.[12] Jurors are also likely to share many of the same belief biases. If we can **link** the facts of our case to the jurors' belief biases, we not only enhance the jurors' ability to accurately perceive, process, and remember the evidence, we also increase the likelihood that they will actually *believe* it.[13] Predictably, jurors find new information more credible if they can relate it to their own idiosyncratic world view and life experiences.

The best way to identify these commonly shared biases is by conducting focus groups. Although not always predictive of the ultimate outcome at trial, focus group results are always instructive. For cases that don't merit the added cost, however, knowing what the most common biases are can help us predict, with a higher degree of accuracy, how our particular jurors are likely to respond to our particular case facts.

---

11. People do try to correct for their biases when they're aware of them and when they fear their biases might affect their judgments negatively. Sometimes, they even over-correct. Duane T. Wegener & Richard E. Petty, *The Flexible Correction Model: The Role of Naïve Theories of Bias in Bias Correction,* 29 ADVANCES IN EXPER. SOC. PSYCHOL. 141–208 (1997); Leonard L. Martin, *Set/Reset: Use and Disuse of Concepts in Impression Formation,* 51 J. PERSONALITY & SOC. PSYCHOL. 493–504 (1986).
12. Norbert L. Kerr et al., *Bias in Judgment: Comparing Individuals and Groups,* 103 PSYCH. REV. 687, 687–89 (1996).
13. Eliot R. Smith & Sarah Queller, *Mental Representations, in* SOCIAL COGNITION 5–27 (Marilyn Brewer et al, eds.) (2004).

II. Cognitive Biases That Affect Juror "Trial Story" Construction

Before we discuss how to successfully link our case to juror belief biases, we must understand what the most common biases are and how they affect juror trial stories and decision-making. The following cognitive and motivational biases play a critical role in juror trial story construction.

A. The Confirmation Bias

The **confirmation bias** is closely related to belief perseverance and biased assimilation. It simply acknowledges that all of us have a decided preference for continuing to believe what we already believe.[14]

It's difficult for us to process information that doesn't fit comfortably into our existing cognitive framework, therefore, we're prone to ignore or be highly skeptical of things that we have little informational or experiential basis for dealing with. This is also why changing our belief biases is so hard: it generates severe cognitive dissonance that we find difficult to resolve.[15]

Psychological experiments have shown that our perceptions are not only influenced by **cognitive factors**, i.e., our preexisting beliefs and expectations—but by **motivational factors** such as hopes, desires, and emotional attachments as well.[16] As a result, our hopes and expectations actually shape our experiences as well as our memory of those experiences.[17] For example, if we attend a sporting event and our team loses a close call, we're more likely to fault the referee than one of our players because we see exactly what we expect and hope to see to avoid cognitive dissonance.

We also "feed" our biases. This is why we like to associate with people who think and act like we do. It's why we prefer watching one television news network over another. For example, people who like to watch Fox News don't usually enjoy watching MSNBC. Although both networks provide news and information, each does so with a particular political bias. We tend to choose the network that confirms our belief biases.

---

14.   Charles G. Lord et al, *Biased Assimilation and Attitude Polarization: The Effects of Prior Theories on Subsequently Considered Evidence,* 37 J. PERSONALITY & SOC. PSYCHOL. 2098 (1979).

15.   Loren J. Chapman & Jean Chapman, *Illusory Correlations as an Obstacle to the Use of Valid Psychodiagnostic Tests,* 74 J. ABNORMAL PSYCHOL. 271–80 (1969); Mark Snyder, *When Belief Creates Reality, in* 18 ADVANCES IN EXPER. SOC. PSYCHOL., 247–305 (L. Berkowitz, ed. 1984).

16.   DOUGLAS A. BERNSTEIN ET. AL., PSYCHOLOGY 18 (8th ed. 2008).

17.   Edward R. Hirt, *Do I See Only What I Expect? Evidence for an Expectancy-Guided Retrieval Model,* 58 J. PERSONALITY & SOC. PSYCHOL. 937–51 (1990); Michael Conway & Michael Ross, *Getting What You Want by Revising What You Had,* 47 J. PERSONALITY & SOC. PSYCHOL. 738 (1984).

At trial, the confirmation bias has a powerful influence on juror story construction. Jurors tend to look for and give disproportionate weight to evidence that confirms their preexisting beliefs rather than honestly and objectively evaluating all the facts. In other words, they don't use the confirmation bias to confirm what *actually* happened, they use it to confirm what they believe *usually* happens or what they *want to believe* actually happened. This means that jurors are likely to reject a trial story that doesn't comport with what they believe or want to believe is true, and instead they replace it with a story of their own that is more consistent with their belief biases.

Some juror reactions to the evidence may surprise us. For example, an ophthalmologist was indicted for eighty-one counts of Medicare fraud for doing unnecessary cataract surgery on elderly patients. The prosecution had a strong case because the surgeries were clearly unnecessary. The defense attorney was justifiably worried that his sixty-two-year-old client would receive a long prison sentence, so he decided to hire a trial consultant.

The trial consultant conducted a series of focus groups before trial. Participants initially convicted the ophthalmologist until several new facts were added. When the trial consultant advised the defense lawyer to begin his opening statement with these new facts, the lawyer was incredulous. He nearly rejected the consultant's advice out of hand because he was planning to fight hard to keep this information from the jury. However, when these new facts were added, focus group participants had exonerated the defendant every time.

Based on the consultant's advice, this is how the defense attorney began his opening statement at trial:

> Dr. Stanton and his wife are incredibly wealthy. They have four lavish homes, both in the United States and abroad. They have an apartment here in New York City, right on Fifth Avenue facing Central Park. They have 400-acre ranch in Montana. They own a beachfront home on the South Pacific island of Fiji. And they have a large villa in the south of France. They also have over $40 million in other assets.

Evidence of the couple's incredible wealth filled a significant gap in the Government's case. Yes, the surgeries were unnecessary, but what was the defendant's motive? Why would a doctor with so much money intentionally commit Medicare fraud? This simply made no sense to jurors when they realized how wealthy the defendant was, so they acquitted him.[18]

---

18. Thanks to attorney Jim Lees of Charleston, West Virginia, who served as the trial consultant in the case on which these facts are very loosely based.

Because the Government didn't answer this question, jurors provided their own answer. They created their own trial story, which confirmed their belief biases about how wealthy people typically behave. They didn't believe that a fabulously wealthy doctor would intentionally defraud Medicare because it simply wasn't worth the risk to someone like him.

If the defense attorney had tried this case without the benefit of pretrial focus groups, the result would have probably been different. By ferreting out the belief biases of potential jurors before trial, however, he was able to create a trial story that confirmed exactly what jurors needed to believe in order to find his client not guilty. This is how we make the confirmation bias work to our advantage. (This case is also an excellent example of the **normative bias** discussed infra in chapter seven.)

B. The Hindsight Bias

> *"You acted unwisely," I cried, "As you see*
> *By the outcome." He calmly eyed me:*
> *"When choosing the course of my action," said he,*
> *"I had not the outcome to guide me."*
>
> *Ambrose Bierce* [19]

The **hindsight bias** causes us to believe a certain outcome is inevitable—*if* we know what the outcome is in advance.[20] This widely recognized phenomenon is pervasive at trial, where the normal method of storytelling is turned on its head.

The hindsight bias significantly affects juror trial story construction. As soon as the trial begins, jurors are told who the parties are and why they're in court. This means they're in the unique position of knowing how our story ends *before* we have an opportunity to tell it. Because they mentally unpack the underlying event in reverse chronological order, their trial stories essentially begin at the ending and move forward from there. Each new piece of information they hear is inadvertently, but inevitably shaped and biased by knowledge of the outcome, particularly with regard to causation.[21]

Advance knowledge of the outcome leads jurors to exaggerate its inevitability and overestimate their own ability to have predicted it in advance. In other words, the hindsight bias causes jurors to think the outcome was

---

19. Barry Goldman, The Science of Settlement 171–72 (2009) (*quoting* Ambrose Bierce).
20. Baruch Fischoff, *Hindsight is Not Equal to Foresight: The Effect of Outcome Knowledge on Judgment under Uncertainty,* 1 J. Experimental Psychol.: Human Perception & Performance 288–89 (1975).
21. Richard Thaler, *Mental Accounting and Consumer Choice,* 4 Marketing Science 199–214 (1985).

inevitable, obvious, and predictable from the start. This makes it easier for them to blame one or both of the parties for failing to anticipate and avoid the harm that now seems so eminently foreseeable.[22]

Although this clairvoyant talent tends to manifest itself belatedly, jurors are no less convinced they could have foreseen the adverse consequences had they been in the same situation as the parties. Jurors quickly forget that the parties didn't have the benefit of hindsight at the time the underlying event actually happened.[23]

1. Hindsight and Counterfactual Thinking

Counterfactual thinking often goes hand in hand with the hindsight bias. (*See* chapter seven on heuristics for a more detailed description.) **Counterfactual thinking** involves mentally simulating or imagining alternatives to reality and playing out the consequences in our minds.[24] Whenever something bad happens for no apparent reason, our belief in a just world and the illusion of control motivate us to automatically "undo" the bad outcome by imagining more palatable alternatives to reality.[25] It's simply easier and less upsetting to imagine what would have, could have, or should have happened than to confront the frightening reality of what actually did happen.[26]

At trial, jurors rely on a self-protective form of counterfactual thinking to explain why the underlying adverse event was allowed to happen. In determining causation, particularly in cases that involve serious injury or death, jurors tend to automatically "undo" the bad thing that happened to the plaintiff by imagining alternative and usually more positive outcomes: "If only the plaintiff had . . . ." Jurors use counterfactual thinking to add or delete facts that create a more palatable, albeit imaginary, ending to the story of our case. Unfortunately, counterfactual thinking tends to exacerbate the hindsight bias.[27]

---

22.   Jonathan Baron & John C. Hershey, *Outcome Bias in Decision Evaluation*, 54 J. Personality & Soc. Psychol. 569–79 (1988).

23.   Fischoff, *supra* note 20, at 288; Frederic Bartlett, Remembering: An Experimental and Social Study (2d ed. 1995).

24.   Daniel Kahneman & Amos Tversky, *The Simulation Heuristic, in* Judgment under Uncertainty: Heuristics and Biases 201–08 (Daniel Kahneman et al, eds. 1982).

25.   *See generally,* Melvin J. Lerner, The Belief in a Just World: A Fundamental Delusion (1980); Ellen J. Langer, *The Illusion of Control*, 32 J. Personality & Soc. Psychol. 311 (1975).

26.   Neal J. Roese & James M. Olson, *Counterfactual Thinking: A Critical Overview, in* What Might Have Been: The Social Psychology of Counterfactual Thinking, 1–55 (Neil J. Roese & James M. Olson, eds. 1995).

27.   Neal J. Roese & James M. Olson, *Counterfactuals, Causal Attributions, and the Hindsight Bias: A Conceptual Integration*, 32 J. Experimental & Soc. Psychol. 197 (1996).

For example, consider the following story crafted by attorneys David Wenner and Greg Cusimano:

> Mr. Jones was forty-seven years old, a father of three, and a successful banking executive. His wife had been ill at home for several months. On the day of the incident, Mr. Jones left his office at the regular time. He sometimes left early to take care of chores at home at his wife's request, but this was not necessary that day.
>
> Mr. Jones did not drive home by his regular route. The day was an exceptionally clear one, and Mr. Jones told his friends in the office that he would drive along the shore to enjoy the view.
>
> The accident occurred at a major intersection. The light turned yellow as Mr. Jones approached. The witness noticed that Jones braked hard to stop at the crossing, although he could easily have gone through. His family recognized this as a common occurrence when Mr. Jones was driving.
>
> As the witness began to cross the street after the light changed, a light truck sped through intersection and landed on Mr. Jones' car from the left. Mr. Jones was killed instantly. It was later ascertained that the truck was driven by a teenage boy who was under the influence of alcohol.
>
> As so commonly happens in such situations, the Jones family and friends often thought and said "If only . . ." during the days after the accident.[28]

Inevitably, we think to ourselves: "If only Mr. Jones had taken his regular route home. If only he had left the office early. If only he hadn't stopped at the light. If only he didn't drive like this." Very few people initially say: "If only that drunk teenager hadn't been drinking and driving."

This simple example illustrates the effect of the hindsight bias, counterfactual thinking, primacy, and the **availability heuristic** (discussed in chapter eight). If jurors begin the trial with knowledge of how their trial stories must end, they begin crafting these trial stories immediately and focus on whatever information we first make available to them. (This is also an example of primacy and recency.)

Here, the story begins with Mr. Jones, so we tend to create counterfactuals about him and what he did and what he should have done instead. Our "if onlys" deal with him instead of the drunk driver who killed him. Obviously, these psychological concepts have a powerful effect on our perceptions.

---

28.   David Wenner & Greg Cusimano.

2. Blaming the Last Actor

When a series of events end badly, people naturally tend to blame **the last actor** for the bad outcome.[29] Take, for example, a star athlete who plays a great basketball game, but misses the last shot before the buzzer sounds. If his team loses by only one point, we tend to fault him for his team's loss, completely forgetting how well he played earlier. We say to ourselves, "If only he hadn't missed that shot, his team would have won."

Whenever we engage in counterfactual thinking, we usually focus on undoing the most recent event (the recency effect).[30] This causes us to focus on undoing the conduct of the last actor as we mentally deconstruct what happened. We find ourselves wondering what the last actor would, could, or should have done differently.

Jurors do the same thing at trial. Because they reason backward from the last causative event, this is usually where their trial stories stop. Jurors don't have to figure out *what* happened, but merely *why* it happened and *who* was responsible.

The hindsight bias leads jurors to construct their personal trial stories with an inordinate emphasis on causation. This makes them more inclined to blame the last actor in the chain of events leading up to the injury. It also makes them prone to overestimate the last actor's ability to foresee and avoid what was about to happen.

The liability portion of a civil trial story generally ends with the injury to the plaintiff, just as the basketball game ends with the star athlete missing the last critical shot of the game. Because jurors know the outcome in advance, it's easy for them to imagine that the plaintiff was the last actor who either caused the bad outcome or failed to take the requisite steps to avoid the harm that seems so predictable in hindsight[31]—even though it may have been inevitable at that point. Obviously, this poses a greater challenge for plaintiff's counsel than for the defense.

If we represent the plaintiff at trial, we need to be particularly aware of how counterfactual thinking can affect the jurors' perceptions of the evi-

---

29. Dale T. Miller & Saku Gunasegaram, *Temporal Order and the Perceived Mutability of Events: Implications for Blame Assignment,* 59(6) J. PERSONALITY & SOC. PSYCHOL. 1111–18 (Dec. 1990).

30. Ruth M.J. Byrne et al, *The Temporality Effect in Counterfactual Thinking about What Might Have Been,* 28 MEMORY & COGNITION, 264–81 (2000); Dale T. Miller & Saku Gunasegaram, *Temporal Order and the Perceived Mutability of Events: Implications for Blame Assignment,* 59 J. PERSONALITY & SOC. PSYCHOL. 1111–18 (1990); Clare R. Walsh & Ruth M.J. Byrne, *Counterfactual Thinking: The Temporal Order Effect,* 32 MEMORY & COGNITION 369–78 (2004).

31. Nyla R. Branscombe et al, *Counterfactual Thinking, Blame Assignment, and Well-Being in Rape Victims,* 25 BASIC & APPLIED SOC. PSYCHOL. 265 (2003).

dence. Because their instinctive reaction to what happened is based on the fear of suffering a similar fate, they tend to mentally "undo" the bad outcome in a way that reconciles what happened with their belief in a just world. Unfortunately, this may cause them to judge the injured plaintiff's conduct more harshly than the defendant's, particularly if the defendant's conduct was negligent rather than intentional or reckless. In attempting to "protect" themselves from similar harm, jurors may automatically blame the party who was unable to protect herself. Unfortunately, this sort of "protection" does nothing to protect or rehabilitate the person who suffered the most.

For example, jurors don't want to imagine having cancer. It's even more repellent for them to imagine that their own physicians could misdiagnose their cancer. In such cases, jurors are likely to create the following counter-factuals: "*If only* the plaintiff had sought a second (or third or fourth) opin-ion, she would have known the lump in her breast was cancerous." "*If only* she had kept herself in better overall physical health, this wouldn't have happened." "*If only* she had been a better person, she wouldn't have gotten cancer."

Jurors' fear of confronting their own mortality leads them to try to con-vince themselves that what happened to the plaintiff could never happen to them. This may cause them to *presume* the plaintiff was careless or irrespon-sible, even if there's no evidence to support that presumption. The jurors' un-conscious need to justify what happened and feel better about their own risk of injury may simply overpower their objectivity and skew their judgment.

C. The Self-Serving Bias

> "*That's the news from Lake Wobegon, where all the women are strong, the men are good-looking, and all the children are above average.*"
> Garrison Keillor

All of us tend to have inflated opinions of our own abilities.[32] This so-called **self-serving bias** is a form of **attributional bias** that causes us to take personal credit for our successes and blame others or external circumstances for our failures. (*See* chapter six on social and attributional biases.) The self-serving bias is particularly pronounced in American culture because we're such a highly individualistic society.[33]

---

32. Youngme Moon, *Don't Blame the Computer: When Self-Disclosure Moderates the Self-Serving Bias.* 13 J. CONSUMER PSYCHOL. 125 (2003).

33. Amy H. Mezulis et al, *Is There a Universal Positivity Bias in Attributions? A Meta-Analytic Review of Individual, Developmental, and Cultural Differences in the Self-Serving Attributional Bias*, 130 PSYCHOL. BULL. 711 (2004).

To ensure that jurors will fairly determine causation and assign blame, we need to understand how they're likely to view themselves in relation to the litigants. Jurors tend to construct their personal trial stories in ways that promote their self-esteem. Whenever they imagine how their own conduct would compare to that of the litigants, they tend to use their **ideal self** rather than their **actual self** as a measuring stick.

Jurors are reluctant to acknowledge that their actual self would have behaved exactly as the plaintiff did. Thanks to the benefit of hindsight, jurors are able to envision how their ideal self would have avoided injury by being braver, stronger, and smarter than the plaintiff. In the process, they may automatically alter their perceptions of the facts without realizing what they're doing.

Psychologists wryly refer to this innate tendency to give ourselves more credit than we give others as the **better-than-average effect**.[34] Obviously, no one is better than average in every respect. Nevertheless, we cling to the belief that we generally *are* better than most people to perpetuate our belief in a just world and the illusion of control.

Maintaining a positive self-image allows us to feel more comfortable with ourselves and other people.[35] Everyone enjoys feeling smart, attractive, and intelligent. Even though we don't always live up to this image of our "ideal" or "better-than-average self," self-serving biases help us protect our self-esteem and fill our innate need to have others think well of us.[36]

To maintain the belief that we're inherently good, better-than-average people, we occasionally have to alter our self-perception as well as our perceptions of others. For example, whenever something bad happens to us, we rarely blame our actual selves. Instead, our "ideal self," the self we want and aspire to be, either looks for someone else to blame or attributes the bad outcome to circumstances beyond our control.

D. The False Consensus Effect

The **false consensus effect** leads us to project our own actions and beliefs onto other people by presuming they think like we do.[37] This self-serving bias affects how we interpret and evaluate information by causing us to exag-

---

34. Mark D. Alicke et al, *Personal Contact, Individuation, and the Better-than-Average Effect,* 68 J. Personality & Soc. Psychol., 804–25 (1995).
35. Daniel T. Gilbert et al., *Looking Forward to Looking Backward: The Misprediction of Regret,* 15 Psychol. Sci. 346–50 (2004).
36. Ross et al, *supra* note 6.
37. Lee Ross et al., *The False Consensus Effect: An Egocentric Bias in Social Perception and Attribution Processes,* 13 J. Experimental & Soc. Psychol., 279–301 (1977).

gerate the probability that others agree with us; indeed, we're often surprised to discover that they don't.[38]

The false consensus effect is ubiquitous at trial. As lawyers, we generally overestimate how well jurors understand what we're trying to say. "*I know what I mean*, so *you jurors* should, too" isn't a workable trial strategy. We must constantly remind ourselves that jurors don't necessarily perceive the evidence as we do—nor as we intend them to. Even if they do, they may remain unconvinced.

For example, both we and our jurors see and hear the same evidence, yet each one of us forms a different mental picture of what actually happened. Our job is to ensure that everyone shares the same mental picture of what happened. This is one of many reasons that using simple, precise language and easy-to-understand exhibits are indispensible components of a well-tried case. Nevertheless, the huge disparity between how much we know about the case and how little jurors know makes it difficult for us to appreciate their perspectives and how hard they must work to make sense of the evidence.

Jurors fall prey to the false consensus effect as well. During deliberations, for example, they're often shocked to find that their fellow jurors may have completely different perceptions of what happened in the case.[39]

E. The Consequences of Leaving Gaps in Our Proof

By the time our case goes to trial, we've lived with the evidence for weeks, months, or even years. Because we're so intimately familiar with the facts and the law, it's easy for us to mistakenly presume that we've told jurors all they need to know and that they understand it the way we want them to.

We cannot fall prey to the false consensus effect and presume that jurors' reactions to the evidence will mirror our own. If we leave any gaps in our proof, jurors are unlikely to fill those gaps with "filler" that is consistent with our theory of the case. To the contrary, they will *automatically* fill any gaps in the evidence with their own belief biases.

Jurors tend to believe what they think *must have happened* as an antecedent to the particular bad outcome, regardless of whether it's the *actual*

---

38. Compare this to the related concept of projection. Sigmund Freud defined it as a psychological defense mechanism through which we attribute our own "bad" or negative thoughts and emotions onto others; *i.e.,* we "project" them in order to make them more acceptable to ourselves. We may even deny having such feelings ourselves and simply attribute them to others, perhaps to alleviate the shame we feel about having such thoughts or character traits. Sigmund Freud, *The Interpretation of Dreams, in* 8 THE STANDARD EDITION OF THE COMPLETE PSYCHOLOGICAL WORKS OF SIGMUND FREUD (J. Strachey, ed. 1900).
39. Nancy Pennington & Reid Hastie, *Explanation-Based Decision-Making: Effects of Memory Structure on Judgment,* 14 J. EXPER. PSYCHOL.: LEARNING, MEMORY, AND COGNITION 521–33 (1988).

antecedent. And when they automatically assume facts not in evidence to make their personal trial stories end "properly," they're more likely to misinterpret what happened.

Even during deliberations, jurors spend over half the time reflecting on their own life experiences and how these experiences compare to the case at hand.[40] Although their personal stories may lend context and meaning to the facts and issues in the case, these stories often become the "filler" jurors use to fill gaps in the evidence. Even worse, when jurors share personal stories during deliberations, they may unfairly influence their fellow jurors' decisions as well. This can be particularly dangerous if other jurors come to view the storyteller as their "resident expert" on a particular subject.

Because jurors tend to disregard or alter facts that are contrary to their own life experiences, we need to discover any relevant experiences the might have had during voir dire—a difficult task at best. Such experiences will not necessarily make them good jurors; indeed, just the opposite may be true. It's difficult for us to gauge how a particular experience may have affected a juror or how it may affect the juror's response to similar experiences in the future. Professional trial consultants can provide the best guidance in such matters if the case justifies the cost.

We can't change jurors' core belief biases, regardless of intrinsic merit. We can, however, learn to better recognize how juror beliefs and biases are likely to affect jurors' perceptions of a potential client's case. In some instances, we can redirect the effect of potentially harmful biases by linking them to our case, or better yet, our case to them. (*See* the example of the wealthy ophthalmologist in Section II(A).) Allowing jurors' belief biases and information-processing strategies to guide and inform our trial strategy gives us a much better chance of overcoming jurors' resistance to persuasion and convincing them that our cause is just.[41]

III. Overcoming Juror Biases for the Plaintiff

We can now begin to put several of these interrelated concepts together and see how they play out at trial. For example, as counsel for the injured plaintiff, we have the distinct advantage of presenting our evidence first. We know that jurors will unconsciously want to "undo" the bad outcome our client suffered to allay their fear of suffering a similar outcome. Their primal need for protection, their belief in a just world, the illusion of control, and the hindsight bias all coalesce to create severe cognitive dissonance whenever we ask jurors to confront their own inherent vulnerability.

---

40. Eric Oliver, The Facts Can't Speak for Themselves (2005).

41. Julia R. Zuwerink & Patricia G. Devine, *Attitude Importance, Forewarning of Message Content, and Resistance to Persuasion*, 22 Basic & Applied Soc. Psychol. 19 (2000).

The easiest way for jurors to alleviate their dissonance is to imagine the plaintiff somehow deserved what happened. Since their just world only "permits" bad things to happen to bad actors, they assume the plaintiff must have either acted badly or is simply a bad person. (*See* chapter four.) This leads jurors to imagine all the ways the plaintiff could and should have avoided being injured (counterfactual thinking).

The hindsight bias and the illusion of control cause jurors to attribute their knowledge of the ultimate outcome to the plaintiff, so they quickly find fault with her response: "If *I* had been in her shoes, *I* would never have been hurt." (This is also the self-serving bias, which is discussed below.) From where they sit in the courtroom, jurors find it difficult to imagine the plaintiff was unable to foresee what was about to happen and take action to avoid being harmed. (Notice the inherent presumption that she could have controlled the situation in the first place. This is also an example of **defensive attribution** and the **fundamental attribution error** discussed in chapter seven.)

We can lessen the effect of these biases by immediately changing the jurors' point of view and shifting juror scrutiny to the defendant at the outset. Our entire case should be about the defendant and what *he* could have and should have done differently, not about our client. (And if we represent the defendant, we can take full advantage of the jurors' propensity to blame the plaintiff by making our case about her and her mistakes.)

Our opening statement for the plaintiff must discourage jurors from imagining what the plaintiff did wrong by proving, in absolute factual terms, how the defendant was in control of the situation and how he had the ability to prevent or avoid the imminent harm. We should begin by enumerating each of his wrongful acts, using present tense and active voice. Telling our trial story using a simple noun-verb sentence structure with few adjectives or adverbs makes it seem more immediate, vivid, and powerful. It also enhances the defendant's role as the primary actor and direct cause of the underlying harm.

We must clearly identify each alternative course of action the defendant could and should have pursued, either immediately before the plaintiff's injury or in the past when he originally set the potential harm in motion. We essentially have to do the jury's counterfactual thinking for them. Without our assistance, jurors may find it difficult to envision all of the alternatives that were available to the defendant—options he could and should have chosen, but didn't.[42]

---

42.   Edward R. Hirt & Keith D. Markman, *Multiple Explanation: A Consider-an-Alternative Strategy for Debiasing Judgments,* 69 J. OF PERSONALITY & SOC. PSYCHOL. 1069–86 (1995).

This is how we **de-bias** jurors' thinking: by suggesting options they might otherwise fail to consider.[43] Quite simply, we combat juror counterfactual thinking by creating counterfacts of our own. It's the availability of alternatives that make the defendant's conduct seem blameworthy.[44] And best of all, jurors will reach this conclusion on their own. Once that happens, we simply need to articulate these counterfacts once again in closing argument. This is how we provide jurors on our side with concise and effective arguments they can use during deliberations to convince other jurors to take our side.

If we can fairly and professionally frame the defendant's actions or omissions as the product of a conscious decision, he seems all the more culpable:

> Dr. Bark [the defendant] violated the first rule of practicing medicine: always rule out the worst possible diagnosis first. When a woman finds a lump in her breast, the worst possible diagnosis is cancer. A doctor must immediately rule out cancer because it's potentially fatal. All Dr. Bark had to do was a simple needle biopsy. No surgery was required, no hospitalization, no anesthetic—just a five-minute outpatient procedure would have told him what he needed to know: that the lump was cancerous. But Dr. Bark chose not to do a needle biopsy. He decided it wasn't necessary. So he told his patient to get dressed and go home and stop worrying about the lump because it was nothing to worry about.
>
> The patient did exactly as she was told. A year later, she died of breast cancer.

If jurors believe the defendant's actions were the product of a conscious decision, they're much more willing to hold him accountable. Jurors want evidence of intent in civil cases, and this is the best way to provide it in a simple negligence case.

Only after discussing the defendant's blameworthy acts and poor decisions should we address what our client did or didn't do. This encourages jurors to believe that the plaintiff's actions were directed solely toward *avoiding* harm rather than *creating* it.

Whenever the people we trust to protect us from harm—people like physicians—fail to live up to our expectations, we're quick to hold them

---

43. Paul Slovic & Baruch Fischhoff, *On the Psychology of Experimental Surprises,* 3 J. Experimental Psychol: Human Perception & Performance 544 (1977).
44. Edward R. Hirt & Keith D. Markman, *Multiple Explanation: A Consider-an-Alternative Strategy for Debiasing Judgments,* 69 J. of Personality & Soc. Psychol. 1069–86 (1995).

accountable because they've shattered our notion of a just world.[45] Jurors feel the same way. If the defendant in question is a professional and the plaintiff is not, we should stress how the defendant's superior knowledge demands that he be held to a higher standard of care: "Who was in a better position to control the outcome—the surgeon wielding the scalpel or the patient under anesthesia?"

IV. Knowing When Juror Biases Cannot Be Overcome

There are many potential plaintiffs who have been seriously injured and deserve compensation, but their cases cannot be successfully tried and won. For example, presume that a potential plaintiff has been diagnosed with and treated for testicular cancer. After the initial round of treatment is completed, one of his testicles swells to the size of a baseball.

The plaintiff reports the swelling to his oncologist. The oncologist tells him not to be alarmed and assures him that swelling is not unusual and is no indication that the cancer has spread. Unfortunately, the oncologist is wrong.

Because the plaintiff likes and trusts his oncologist, he doesn't seek a second opinion. He delays further treatment and only returns to his oncologist after the cancer has spread and the prognosis is dire. The plaintiff finally consults a lawyer, but even then, he's initially reluctant to file suit against his doctor.

This case is likely to pose insurmountable problems at trial. Before we agree to take the case, we must consider how jurors are likely to view the evidence. When the trial begins, jurors will know that the plaintiff's cancer has recurred and spread. The hindsight bias causes them to think that they would have immediately recognized pronounced testicular swelling as symptomatic of a recurrence of the cancer. Once they've convinced themselves the plaintiff was probably at fault, they begin to imagine all the ways they would have behaved differently than the plaintiff:

> If *I* had been in the plaintiff's shoes, I would have known that an enlarged testicle is a sure sign of cancer. If *my* oncologist had told me there was nothing to worry about, I wouldn't have listened to him. *I* would have demanded treatment immediately or asked for a referral to another oncologist. If my doctor refused, *I* would have found another oncologist on my own. If

---

45. Former President Bill Clinton and former New York governor Eliot Spitzer are prime examples of this. We needed to perceive them as "good" because we entrusted them with important leadership positions. When they later exhibited characteristics we disapproved of and we discovered our unreasonable perceptions and expectations were wrong, we turned on them and attacked them with a vengeance.

that didn't work, *I* would have gone to my family doctor and demanded an immediate referral. Or *I* would have gone to the emergency room. And *I* would have persisted until I was successfully treated for cancer. That's why this could never happen to *me.*

The plaintiff's lawyer ultimately told him the case could not be won.[46] The lawyer knew that jurors would ask themselves the questions above, many of which were unanswerable. (Remember, however, that you are ethically required to urge that client to get a second opinion.)

Before we agree to take a case, we must mentally run through a "counterfactual checklist" to determine how prospective jurors may perceive the evidence. It's important to spend time at the outset thinking about how jurors are likely to react to the facts on both a conscious and unconscious level. The hierarchy of juror decision-making can help us determine if a case can be won.

Sadly, we must often reconcile ourselves with the reality that there are many deserving plaintiffs who won't receive adequate compensation for their injuries. Our job is to settle these cases if we can and decline to take them if we can't.

---

46. Thanks to Tom Comerford of Comerford & Britt in Winston-Salem, North Carolina, for sharing this real-life story.

CHAPTER SIX

SOCIAL BIASES: ATTRIBUTION THEORY

I. Introduction

Human beings are very social creatures. We spend an inordinate amount of time thinking about ourselves and trying to evaluate our thoughts, feelings, and abilities relative to those of other people. We also ponder why other people behave as they do and why events unfold in a particular way. These **social comparisons** give us a better sense of who we are by giving us some idea of the correctness of our opinions, the strength of our abilities, and many other things.[1]

We rely on our **social perceptions** to understand and make judgments about other people so we can decide how to properly react to them.[2] Unfortunately, we often misinterpret **social information**, which can bias our perceptions and cause us to react inappropriately or unwisely.

Social biases play a pivotal role in juror decision-making and are closely related to all of the biases discussed in the preceding chapter. Since many social and cognitive biases work in conjunction with one another, it's nearly impossible to separate their application at trial. (This chapter should be read in conjunction with the last, because it builds on all of the concepts we've just discussed.)

Although we expect jurors to be impartial, they are not immune to social biases. Their own self-concepts (which may bear little relation to reality) play a significant role in how they evaluate the conduct of the litigants and determine causation. Unfortunately, the egocentric standards that jurors use to make social comparisons are often inaccurate and can adversely influence their perceptions of our case.

---

1. Joanne V. Wood & Kathryn L. Taylor, *Serving Self-Relevant Goals through Social Comparison, in* SOCIAL COMPARISON: CONTEMPORARY THEORY & RESEARCH 23–49 (Jerry M. Suls & Thomas A. Wills, eds. 1991).
2. Bram P. Buunk et al, *Social Comparisons at Work as Related to a Cooperative Social Climate and to Individual Differences in Social Comparison Orientation,* 54 APP. PSYCHOL.: AN INT'L REV. 61–80 (2005).

II. Attributional Biases

Attribution theory is the psychological term that describes how we make causal ascriptions for actions and outcomes. In other words, it's how we attribute or assign control to someone or something. But for our purposes, it's how jurors assign blame or fault.

Because we're innately and insatiably curious to know why things happen and what motivates human behavior (including our own), we automatically try to explain these things to ourselves. Our explanations, however, tend to be biased and self-serving. We usually give ourselves more credit in any given situation than we're willing to give other people; therefore, we tend to judge the conduct of others unfairly by demanding more of them than we normally demand of ourselves.[3]

Our schemata create certain expectations about how people should behave. These expectations, along with our primal need for protection and predictability in life, give rise to various **attributional biases**. It's important for us to be able to **attribute** certain characteristics to ourselves and others to: (1) understand behavior, (2) predict future behavior, and (3) decide how to control or manage prospective behavior.[4] In other words, we need to be able to assume that people's actions have predictable consequences to protect ourselves, maintain sound mental health, and plan for the future.[5] (*See* chapter three on belief in a just world and the illusion of control.) This compels us to make implicit assumptions about why people (including ourselves) behave as they do.

Our explanations for human motivation and causation have a peculiarly personal slant because we automatically use ourselves as a habitual reference point for assessing other people and events. This psychological phenomenon of constantly assessing others in relation to ourselves is called the **self-reference effect**.[6]

Whenever we compare ourselves to others, we generally benefit from the comparison because a variety of **self-serving biases** make us biased in favor of ourselves, particularly when our intellect, personalities, or talents are

---

3. Lee Ross & Richard E. Nisbett, The Person or the Situation: Perspectives of Social Psychology (1991).

4. Scott Plous, The Psychology of Judgment and Decision-making 697 (1993).

5. Melvin J. Lerner, The Belief in a Just World: A Fundamental Delusion 105–11 (1980).

6. T.B. Rogers, *A Model of the Self as an Aspect of the Human Information Processing System, in* Personality, Cognition, and Social Interaction 193–214 (Nancy Cantor & John F. Kihlstrom, eds. 1981); T.B. Rogers et al, *Self-Reference and the Encoding of Personal Information,* 35 J. Personality & Soc. Psychol. 677–88 (1977). *See also* Thomas K. Srull & Lisa Gaelick, *General Principles and Individual Differences in the Self as a Habitual Reference Point: An Examination of Self-Other Judgments of Similarity,* 2 Soc. Cognition, 108–21 (1983).

involved.[7] We tend to *overestimate* how many people share our negative attributes such as fearfulness; but we tend to *underestimate* how many people share our personal strengths.[8]

A related attributional bias, the **egocentric bias**, makes us inclined to claim more credit for positive joint outcomes and behaviors than other contributors and less credit for negative outcomes or behaviors.[9] For example, married couples tend to overestimate their partner's fault in *causing* conflict, yet each will claim more credit for *resolving* it.[10] This may also be due to **availability** rather than mere ego because it's easier for us to retrieve our own actions from memory than those of others.[11] (*See* **availability heuristic** in chapter eight.)

A. The Actor-Observer Bias

In his seminal book, *The Psychology of Interpersonal Relations,* Fritz Heider noted that "behavior engulfs the field [of observation]."[12] This simply means that in a social setting, an observer tends to focus on the actors and their behavior, while everything else seems to fade into the background. This is due, in part, to the powerful influence that visual orientation has on our perception of causation or "causal attributions."[13]

From our point of view as observers, the actor seems to dominate the situation. Therefore, when we instinctively try to explain his behavior to ourselves, it's only natural that we focus on the actor as a *person* rather than the *situation* he's in, because we're seldom aware of what another person's situation might be. Consequently, due to our lack of information the actor's internal or dispositional characteristics seem more **salient** (standing out relative to their surroundings) than his situation or circumstances.

Because we feel compelled to maintain psychological control of our world, we need to believe in our ability to predict what others will do in most situations through observation alone. Therefore, we tend to *presume* that we have sufficient information about the actor as a person, based almost exclusively

---

7.   Dale T. Miller & Michael Ross, *Self-Serving Biases in the Attribution of Causality: Fact or Fiction?,* 82 PSYCHOL. BULL. 213–25 (1975).
8.   Jerry M. Suls & C. K. Wan, *In Search of the False Uniqueness Phenomenon: Fear and Estimates of Social Consensus,* 52 J. PERSONALITY & SOC. PSYCHOL. 211–17 (1987).
9.   Michael Ross & Fiore Sicoly, *Egocentric Biases in Availability and Attribution,* 37 J. PERSONALITY & SOC. PSYCHOL. 322–36 (1979).
10.   *Id.*
11.   Suzanne C. Thompson & Harold H. Kelley, *Judgments of Responsibility for Activities in Close Relationships,* 41 J. PERSONALITY & SOC. PSYCHOL. 469–77 (1981).
12.   FRITZ HEIDER, THE PSYCHOLOGY OF INTERPERSONAL RELATIONS (1958).
13.   Michael D. Storms, *Videotape and the Attribution Process: Reversing Actors' and Observers' Points of View,* 27 J. PERSONALITY & SOC. PSYCHOL. 974–91 (1973).

on our observations. This leads us to rely heavily on **internal or dispositional attributions** to explain the actor's conduct.[14]

Whenever we are actors rather than observers, the converse is true. We tend to think that a person's behavior corresponds with their disposition (**correspondence bias**).[15] Research on attributional biases suggests that we have unrealistic expectations of how a person "should" behave in a given situation, perhaps because we're too busy or unmotivated to correct effortlessly made dispositional attributions by considering the power of the situation.[16]

We don't "observe" ourselves "acting" because we're focused on what we're doing; but we're fully aware of our situation because it's more important to us. Therefore, we tend to explain our own actions in terms of *situational* factors (**external attribution**) rather than personal or dispositional characteristics (**internal attribution**), particularly when our behavior is improper or inappropriate. This psychological phenomenon is known as the **actor-observer bias**.[17]

The actor-observer bias inclines us to make internal attributions for our *own* achievements, but makes us generally unwilling to do the same for others. Whenever we experience a positive outcome, we gladly take full credit for it. For example, if we "ace" an exam, we tend to attribute the good grade to our own intelligence, ability, or inherent "goodness." But if a classmate gets a better grade on the exam than we did, we're likely to presume that he was lucky, had more time to study than we did, or was the teacher's favorite student. The actor-observer bias makes us more inclined to attribute our classmate's good fortune to external attributes rather than any positive internal attributes he may possess.

Simply put, we tend to believe that *we earn positive outcomes* because of our internal attributes while *others earn negative outcomes* because of their internal attributes.[18] Consequently, whether we choose to focus on the person or the situation also tends to be *outcome related.* Therefore, we can sum up the actor-observer bias as follows:

---

14. Edward Jones & Richard E. Nisbett, *The Actor and the Observer: Divergent Perceptions of the Causes of Behavior, in* ATTRIBUTION: PERCEIVING THE CAUSES OF BEHAVIOR (Edward Jones et al, eds. 1971).

15. For a detailed discussion of "correspondence bias," or drawing dispositional inferences for another's behavior that could have been explained by situational factors, *see* Daniel T. Gilbert & Patrick S. Malone, *The Correspondence Bias,* 117 PSYCHOL. BULL. 21–38 (1995).

16. *Id.* Interestingly, there are also situations in which people will inadequately take into account another's disposition when determining the causes of behavior, thereby *overweighing* the situation.

17. Harold H. Kelley, *The Processes of Causal Attribution,* 28 AM. PSYCHOL. 107–28 (1973).

18. LERNER, *supra* note 5, at 105–11.

- *If something good happens to me, I take credit for it. But if something bad happens to me, it's not my fault. It's either someone else's fault or it's simply the situation I was in, which I couldn't control.*

- *When other people have positive outcomes, I'm often unwilling to give them the same credit that I give to myself. If something bad happens to someone else, it's either his own fault or he's probably a bad person who deserved a bad outcome.*

Researchers have found that we tend to succumb to the actor-observer bias less frequently with people we know and like, such as close friends and family. Because we have more information about their needs, motivations and thoughts, we're more likely to account for external forces that may impact their behavior.[19] Since jurors are not allowed to sit in judgment of friends or family members, however, they're unlikely to give the litigants the same benefit of the doubt.

B. The Fundamental Attribution Error

The actor-observer bias is strongest whenever we try to determine why something bad happened to another person. Our tendency to overemphasize internal or dispositional factors when observing others by focusing on the *person* rather than the *situation* is such a strong self-protective bias that it can lead to pervasive errors in judgment. [20] In fact, our inclination to make dispositional attributions is so often patently incorrect that psychologists refer to this propensity as a fundamental "error" rather than a mere "bias," thus the name **fundamental attribution error**.[21]

Whenever other people experience bad outcomes, we tend to overemphasize the role of their personal or internal attributes when deciding what caused the outcome. The fundamental attribution error may cause us to *unjustifiably* attribute someone else's misfortune to their bad character, immorality, or some other personal flaw. We simply presume their behavior was motivated by dispositional causes rather than external or situational causes, although we're rarely aware of what we're doing. This is one of many reasons that jurors may presume the injured plaintiff *must have* done something to deserve her bad outcome.

If we represent the injured plaintiff, we know that the fundamental attribution error may cause jurors to unfairly scrutinize our client's actions or

---

19.   Arthur Aron et al., *Inclusion of the Other in the Self Scale and the Structure of Interpersonal Closeness*, 63 J. PERSONALITY & SOC. PSYCHOL., 596–612 (1992).
20.   Lee Ross, *The Intuitive Psychologist and His Shortcomings: Distortions in the Attribution Process, in* 10 ADVANCES IN EXPERIMENTAL SOCIAL PSYCHOLOGY (Leonard Berkowitz, ed. 1977).
21.   Glenn D. Reeder, *Let's Give the Fundamental Attribution Error Another Chance*, 43 J. PERSONALITY & SOC. PSYCHOL. 341–44 (1982).

disposition in an attempt to blame her for what happened. Because jurors tend to see the trial as a morality play, we should make Act I, Scene I (our opening statement) about the "bad" guy so jurors can attribute fault immediately—but not to our client. If our trial story makes the defendant's conduct more salient than the plaintiff's, jurors are more likely to begin their own trial stories with his bad conduct or disposition rather than hers. Otherwise, they may fail to consider the untenable situation the plaintiff was in, as we saw in the examples in the previous chapter.

C. Social Roles

Jurors often draw conclusions at trial based on factors that are largely irrelevant, such as how the "actors" (lawyers, parties, and witnesses) are dressed, where they come from, or what they do for a living. This can happen because jurors are generally unaware of how social information, particularly **social roles**, can affect their perceptions.

Stanford University professor Lee Ross and his colleagues conducted experiments on social roles in which participants were randomly assigned to play the role of contestant or questioner in a "quiz show." When playing the role of questioner, both contestants and questioners perceived the questioner as having superior knowledge relative to contestants—even though everyone knew they were merely role-playing. Ross concluded that people don't usually recognize and correct for the advantages and disadvantages of social roles in a particular situation.[22]

Social roles can affect juror perceptions at trial. For example, most jurors perceive the judge as the smartest person in the courtroom. She sits in an elevated position in the center of the courtroom dressed in a black robe and seems to be in total command of the proceedings. The lawyers are dressed in suits and seem to know what the rules are. This may lead jurors to perceive lawyers as having an unfair social advantage over witnesses.

The "social role" of a criminal defendant is rife with prejudice. Jurors rely on their personal impressions of a stereotypical "criminal defendant" to form behavioral inferences about a particular defendant, however unfair that may be.[23] Even though the Rules of Evidence generally prohibit the use of character evidence to prove conforming conduct, [24] jurors manage to do the same thing, to some extent, through observation of social roles.

---

22.   Lee D. Ross et al., *Social Roles, Social Control and Biases in Social-Perception Processes*, 35 J. Personality & Soc. Psychol. 485–94 (1977).
23.   Denise R. Beike & Steven J. Sherman, *Social Inference: Inductions, Deductions, and Analogies, in* Handbook of Social Cognition (Robert S. Wyer & Thomas K. Srull, eds. 1994).
24.   Fed. R. Evid. 404.

Jurors may also form inferences about social roles based on gender or ethnicity. For example, if a juror believes that all women are lousy mechanics, he's liable to judge the female defendant unfairly by presuming that she negligently repaired the plaintiff's truck.

1. The Attractiveness Bias

Interestingly, appearance seems to matter in any forum. This is due to the **attractiveness bias**.[25] All of us find it difficult to perceive another person as a composite of many separate qualities, each with its own relative value, independent of the others. We automatically tend to associate positive character traits with physically attractive people due to the **halo effect**.[26]

Jurors frequently fall prey to the attractiveness bias at trial. More attractive litigants have an inherent advantage, at least initially, over unattractive ones, simply because the attractiveness bias is so pervasive in our society. This is one of the reasons that it's so important for us and our clients to present our "best selves" to the jury.

2. An Illusory Perception of Competence

Social roles and self-serving biases may cause us to presume that people whom we trust to protect us are competent and trustworthy. We have a deep-seated need to preserve our confidence in those we trust to care for and protect the general public. This may lead us to believe, for example, that our pharmacist will accurately fill our prescriptions or that car manufacturers will build safe and reliable cars for us to drive.

An illusion of competence may also lead us to presume that a white lab coat with a name on it is sufficient proof of a doctor's or pharmacist's competence or that thieves dressed in movers' uniforms and driving a moving van are "authorized" to load up our neighbor's belongings and drive away with them. These presumptions are based on pure observation. If the "actors" look and act the part, we simply presume they're competent.

Although these perceptions of competence may be objectively inaccurate, we need to believe we've chosen our "protectors" wisely and that we can't be fooled. This presumption is a logical extension of the belief in a just world and, perhaps, the illusion of control. Part of being able to predict and control outcomes in life includes being able to gauge the character and competence of others, particularly those we entrust with our health or well-being. This is how we avoid taking needless risks that could compromise our safety.

25.   Kenneth Dion et al., *What Is Beautiful Is Good,* 24 J. PERSONALITY & SOC. PSYCHOL. 285–90 (1972).
26.   Edward L. Thorndike, *A Constant Error in Psychological Ratings,* 4 J. APPLIED PSYCH. 25–29 (1920).

These presumptions are related to Stanley Milgram's famous obedience to authority studies in which participants were asked to shock "learners" (who were actors working with the experimenter) at increasingly high voltages.[27] Participants continued to administer the shocks, even after the learners screamed in pain and begged the participants to stop. Participants continued to do as they were told in blind obedience to the experimenter's authority, simply because they presumed the experimenter would not allow them to permanently injure the learners. Had the learners not been paid actors who were never actually harmed, the consequences of presuming the experimenter's competence might have been serious.[28]

Whenever seemingly "reliable" people turn out to be less reliable than we'd hoped, we're disappointed and frustrated with them, largely because they've failed to live up to our own inflated expectations of competence.[29] We may even feel a sense of moral outrage, because to admit that we trusted the wrong people creates severe cognitive dissonance.

III. Attributional Errors at Trial

At trial, jurors are "observers" who must evaluate the past conduct of the parties who were "actors" in the unfortunate event that brought them to court. Because this is the type of situation in which attributional biases are quite powerful, jurors are likely to attribute the bad outcome to dispositional rather than situational factors. In other words, *jurors tend to link character traits to the parties' conduct and ignore the context in which their behavior occurred.*[30] Since attributional bias is outcome-related, the party who has suffered most—the person who had a bad outcome—is the easiest person to blame. And that's usually the injured plaintiff.

A. Defensive Attribution

Jurors, to varying extents, need their "just world" to be neat, predictable, and orderly, and there's little we can do to change such a mindset. The idea that the plaintiff was an innocent victim of someone else's wrongdoing or negligence creates severe cognitive dissonance because jurors don't want to believe that someone has suffered undeservedly.

In the last chapter, we saw how jurors inject themselves into the trial by deciding how they—or, more accurately, how their *ideal selves*—would have

27. Stanley Milgram, *Behavioral Study of Obedience,* 67 J. ABNORMAL & SOC. PSYCHOL. 371–78 (1963).
28. Thomas Blass, *The Milgram Paradigm after 35 Years: Some Things We Now Know about Obedience to Authority,* 29 J. APPLIED SOC. PSYCHOL. 955–78 (1999).
29. Prime examples are former president Richard Nixon and 2008 presidential candidate John Edwards.
30. ROSS & NISBETT, *supra* note 3.

behaved if they were in the same situation as the parties. This is the self-reference effect, which causes jurors to make decisions by imagining how they would have behaved in the same situation. In their personal trial stories, they inevitably put themselves in the position of the party who suffered a bad outcome to figure out why it happened.

Because jurors see themselves as "good" people who don't deserve a bad outcome, their personal trial stories *cannot* have unhappy endings. They don't even want to consider the prospect of being injured. This is why jurors' trial stories center around how they would have "dodged the bullet" that "wounded" the plaintiff—how they could "undo" the bad thing that happened to her. Then they begin to wonder why she couldn't have done the same: "Why couldn't *she* have been a superhero like me [in my imagination] and come out of this situation unscathed?"

Jurors may reconcile what happened to the plaintiff by convincing themselves that no injustice has occurred, which immediately alleviates their cognitive dissonance.[31] The easiest way for them to make things "right" may be to attribute blame for the bad outcome to the injured plaintiff herself, a tendency referred to as **defensive attribution**.[32] Unfortunately, the only people this cognitive strategy "defends" are the jurors themselves, who aren't in any danger of actual harm.

If jurors presume the plaintiff behaved badly or simply got what she deserved, they can successfully "defend" themselves against the thought of suffering similar harm and make their world seem just once again.[33] Unfortunately, it's easier for them to denigrate the plaintiff and create emotional distance from her than to carefully sort out what actually happened, as we've seen in previous examples.[34]

Defensive attribution actually illustrates just-world effects by inclining jurors to blame the victim to avoid feeling that they could be "victimized" themselves.[35] This tendency can lead jurors to judge the conduct of the injured plaintiff more harshly than that of the defendant by presuming she was irresponsible, inattentive, or somehow to blame for her own injury.

---

31.   LERNER, *supra* note 5, at 9–17.
32.   Jerry M. Burger, *Motivational Biases in the Attribution of Responsibility for an Accident: A Meta-Analysis of the Defensive Attribution Hypothesis,* PSYCHOL. BULL., 96 J. OF PERSONALITY & SOC. PSYCHOL. 496–512 (1981). *See also* David A. Wenner & Gregory S. Cusimano, *Combating Juror Bias,* TRIAL, 30 (June 2000).
33.   Burger, *supra* note 32.
34.   *Id.*
35.   *Id. See also* Nathan Radcliffe & William Klein, *Dispositional, Unrealistic, and Comparative Optimism: Differential Relations with the Knowledge and Processing of Risk Information and Beliefs about Personal Risk,* 28 PERSONALITY & SOC. PSYCHOL. BULL. 836–46 (2002).

Interestingly, the more a particular juror has in common with the plaintiff, the more likely he is to attribute what happened to her actions or bad character.[36] The unique ability to identify with the plaintiff's unfortunate situation makes the juror want to put even more psychological distance between them. This is why women are not usually good jurors in breast cancer cases. They're often too frightened of the disease themselves to empathize with the injured plaintiff.

In jurors' counterfactual scenarios, they imagine what their ideal selves (rather than their actual selves) would have done that the plaintiff did not. "She had a bad outcome. Let me think of all the ways that I could have avoided it if I were in her shoes." Hindsight and defensive attribution insure that, in their imagination, jurors will inevitably behave better than the plaintiff did. The risk is that jurors may later use these imaginary counterfactuals to form opinions and draw inferences and conclusions that are totally unsupported by the evidence, never realizing that they're confusing fact with fantasy in their contaminated memory.[37]

B. The Illusion of Professional Competence

An illusory presumption of competence makes jurors reluctant to believe that the plaintiff was actually injured by the negligence of a seemingly "competent" professional. If the defendant who allegedly caused the plaintiff's harm is someone jurors trust to take care of them and protect them, they're more likely to find that the defendant acted competently. Their fear of being left unprotected by someone they trust—someone like the defendant—may cause them to automatically discount the possibility that he could have failed to protect the plaintiff. If jurors unwittingly help the defendant live up to their inflated expectations of his competence, this can compromise the plaintiff's case.

For example, in a products liability suit against a car manufacturer, jurors are reluctant to believe that the defendant would make defective automobiles that could cause harm to innocent drivers. Jurors themselves drive cars. Their children ride in their cars. Therefore, they need to believe their cars are safe and reliable, so they're reluctant to find the defendant manufacturer liable.

IV. Overcoming Attributional Biases

Jurors are generally unaware of how attributional biases influence their decision-making. Nevertheless, their propensity to interpret the cause of the

---

36. Berger, *supra* note 32.
37. Vittorio Girotto et al., *Postdecisional Counterfactual Thinking by Actors and Readers,* 18 PSYCHOL. SCI. 510–15 (2007).

parties' behavior as dispositional rather than situational has a significant effect on how they allocate fault.[38]

Attributional biases generally work to the defendant's advantage. Defensive attribution tends to make jurors more inclined to find that the plaintiff's own conduct or disposition was the cause of her injury; therefore, they're likely to scrutinize her conduct or personal characteristics with an eye to finding fault. Obviously, this poses a problem if we represent the plaintiff. We'll need to overcome these obstacles to achieve a just result for our client.

A. Focusing on the Defendant

The same solutions we used to combat juror bias (discussed in chapter five) apply to defensive attribution. For example, we should begin our opening statement for the plaintiff with a purely factual account of the defendant's wrongful acts to show how he personally controlled or created the circumstances or situation that ultimately caused harm to our client. Jurors are more willing to fault action than inaction; in fact, they're naturally inclined to presume intent with action, often intent to produce the particular outcome in question.[39] Therefore, it's more persuasive to prove that the defendant's *actions* caused the harm rather than his *failure to act*.

"Actions" can be as simple as seeing, hearing, or knowing something, particularly if we tell a short, simple, but compelling story:

> He comes from far away. [*Pause.*] Rolls into town in his big white truck. [*Pause.*] He sees her there on the sidewalk—pushing her walker—and he slows down. [*Pause.*] He knows she can't get down in the basement. [*Pause.*] He *likes* what he sees.[40]

Only three short sentences and jurors already know that something bad is about to happen to the plaintiff. They don't even know what happens next, but they're ready to blame the defendant for it. Why?

We've told our story in present tense, which creates intimacy, immediacy, and irresistible forward momentum. Jurors find themselves irresistibly pulled into our story. Why? Because we've used a simple noun-verb sentence structure punctuated by brief, but meaningful pauses. There are no wasted words. The only two adjectives used describe the defendant's truck.

This approach makes it harder for jurors to distance themselves from the defendant's actions, even though they know nothing about who "he" is,

---

38. PLOUS, *supra* note 4, at 181–82.
39. *See generally* ROSS & NISBETT *supra* note 3; ERIC OLIVER, FACTS CAN'T SPEAK FOR THEMSELVES (2005).
40. Thanks to attorney Joseph Anderson of Anderson & Pangia in Winston-Salem, North Carolina, for this piece of a beautiful opening statement.

where he comes from ("far away"), or what he's about to do. They also don't know who "she" is, but already they want to know more.

We'll continue to dole out information in small chunks and tell the story of how "he," the nameless bad guy, convinces "her," the elderly homeowner, that he can repair the sagging foundation of her home—that he's just the man for the job. But even before we say it, jurors know he's going to take her money and bail out before the foundation is properly repaired. So our story will end with only a brief mention of our client:

> Six months went by. [*Pause.*] She paid him over $15,000. [*Pause.*] It was nearly all the money she had. [*Pause.*] And the foundation of her home is still unstable.

Talking about our client and her actions in past tense makes her conduct seem removed from what happened and less blameworthy in comparison to the defendant. Even though we're blaming him for his faulty repair work, we should scrupulously avoid negativity or embellishment, which may cause jurors to discount what we say as unfairly biased in favor of our client.

This simple example demonstrates how we can capitalize on the jurors' tendency to overestimate the role of personality and underestimate situational factors by telling nothing but the simple, elemental story of what the defendant did. Jurors are already inclined to link behavior to character traits. The beginning of our story immediately provides that link, leaving jurors to do the rest. It subtly emphasizes the defendant's dispositional attributes without saying anything specific or negative about his character. This helps neutralize the jury's inclination to scrutinize the plaintiff and her actions.

B. Avoiding Negativity

Throughout trial, we should focus on bad *acts* rather than bad *people*. Unless the opposing party is a truly reprehensible person, ad hominem attacks should generally be avoided, particularly if there is no claim for punitive damages. Jurors' attributional biases will do the job for us, often unfairly so. Besides, unjustified negative judgments about the opposing party hurt our case as well as our credibility.

Any negative opinions or conclusions that need to be drawn should come from the testimony of expert witnesses whenever possible. Experts are free to state opinions and draw inferences and conclusions that lay witnesses cannot. If we later repeat the things our expert said about the opposing party's bad conduct in our closing argument, we're not making the negative judgment ourselves: we're merely referring to what our expert said in sworn testimony, which is a much more palatable approach.

C. Using Options to Infer Intent

Showing that the defendant had options, alternatives, or choices is always powerful evidence of fault. In the example above, our closing argument will not only discuss how the contractor did substandard work, it will also highlight the fact that he deliberately *chose* to solicit work from a trusting, but gullible elderly woman.

If we compare the alternative that the defendant chose with other better alternatives he *could* have chosen but didn't, we can show his disregard for the safety of others and the foreseeability of the harm, both of which make him seem more blameworthy. If jurors believe the defendant's wrongdoing was the product of a conscious decision, they will *infer* that he intended the consequences of his actions. Even though intent is not an element of negligence, the very act of making a decision seems more culpable than making a mistake or failing to act. Each additional alternative we present makes the defendant seem more responsible.

We should compare and contrast the defendant's multiple options with the lack of options available to the plaintiff. Showing that the defendant's conduct left the plaintiff with no viable alternatives highlights both the *dispositional* aspect of his conduct and the *situational* aspect of hers.

Jurors are automatically inclined to look for motive when evaluating the conduct of the parties. If we can legally, morally and professionally show that the defendant had a motive to cause harm or that he acted on purpose or with a purpose, jurors will be more inclined to find that he was responsible for the bad outcome.

D. Using Rules to Show Wrongdoing

Jurors understand the need for rules and are willing to find fault with people who break them.[41] "Rules" can be anything from statutes or ordinances to the policies and procedures of a small business or civic organization. They need not have the force of law to make jurors feel more confident holding the rule-breaker responsible.

If we represent the plaintiff, portraying the defendant as a "rule-breaker" is an effective tactic. Most jurors pride themselves on being people who follow the rules rather than break them. (*See* chapter seven on **normative bias** as well.) For example, in the opening statement above, we could begin with a rule: "A contractor has a duty to do the job properly," or "No one should expect to be paid for work they didn't do."

---

41. *See generally* Rick Friedman & Patrick Malone, Rules of the Road: A Plaintiff's Guide to Proving Liability (2006); David Ball on Damages (3d ed. 2011).

If the defendant's failure to follow the relevant rules was the proximate cause of the plaintiff's injury, even the most conservative jurors will be willing to hold the defendant responsible. Although these sorts of people aren't usually "pro-plaintiff," they see themselves as law-abiding citizens who always follow the rules. This makes them more likely to hold the defendant accountable for his failure to do so.[42]

There are many wonderful examples of how to use this "rule-breaker" frame to the plaintiff's advantage in books like *David Ball on Damages*[43] or Rick Friedman and Patrick Malone's *Rules of the Road*. Friedman and Malone offer many examples like this one from a medical negligence case: "A doctor who is diagnosing a patient's symptoms has a duty to rule out the most dangerous, treatable potential diseases first."[44] This rule is unassailable, even by those in the medical profession.

Be aware, however, that rules can work for both sides. In the example above, the defense can counter with a rule of its own, like: "The best doctor in the world can't effectively treat a patient who refuses to follow the doctor's orders." Even the plaintiff herself can't refute this rule and maintain her credibility.

E. Living in a Just World?

The "just world" theory proposes an inverse correlation between sympathy and blame.[45] Whenever we blame an innocent victim simply to reassure ourselves that we live in a just world, we either distance ourselves from the victim or dehumanize her, both of which defeat compassion.[46] An inverse correlation between sympathy and blame ultimately refutes the notion that justice will always prevail.

The jurors' strong tendency to engage in defensive attribution leads them to blame the victim to assure themselves that they won't become victims in the future.[47] This is, perhaps, the most difficult obstacle for plaintiff's counsel to overcome at trial.

Because jurors tend to overestimate the ability of other people to control their own fate, particularly if they experience a bad outcome, we want to encourage them to overestimate the defendant's ability to control the outcome. This levels the playing field by counteracting a similar tendency to overestimate the plaintiff's ability to control her own fate.

---

42. *Id.*
43. BALL, *supra* note 41.
44. FRIEDMAN & MALONE, *supra* note 41.
45. LERNER, *supra* note 5, at 105–11.
46. RICHARD LAZARUS, EMOTION AND ADAPTATION, 289 (1991).
47. LERNER, *supra* note 5, at 105–11.

CHAPTER SEVEN

CULTURAL NORMS AND BIASES

I. Introduction

All human beings have a need for "belonging."[1] Being part of a particular group or culture is essential to health and personal safety because it allows us to pool our resources, live together in harmony, and advance the collective interests of our "tribe."[2]

Our need to belong causes us to instinctively mimic the behavior of those around us (the members of our "tribe") because we appreciate the need to conform to the **cultural norms** or widely accepted and expected customs, rules, beliefs, and behaviors of our society.[3] We understand that failure to conform will garner the disapproval of others. More serious violations of cultural norms may lead to punishment or even ostracism from our tribe.[4] This provides strong incentive for us to appropriately adapt to the expectations of others around us, a process known as **socialization**.[5]

We assimilate culturally transmitted norms during early childhood, and they continue to exert a powerful influence on our behavior throughout our lives.[6] We rely on cultural norms to interpret behavior, solve problems, and make decisions.[7] We tend to gravitate toward people who share our attitudes, beliefs, and opinions, simply because we feel more comfortable around them. People who think, speak, and act like we do are predictable; therefore, we rarely experience cognitive dissonance or psychological discomfort in their

---

1. Roy F. Baumeister & Mark R. Leary, *The Need to Belong: Desire for Interpersonal Attachments as a Fundamental Human Motivation,* 117 PSYCHOL. BULL. 497–529 (1995).
2. Solomon E. Asch, *Effects of Group Pressure Upon the Modification and Distortion of Judgment, in* GROUPS, LEADERSHIP, AND MEN (Harold Guetzkow, ed. 1951); Solomon E. Asch, *Opinions and Social Pressure,* 193 SCI. AM. 31–35 (1955); IRVING L JANUS, GROUPTHINK: A PSYCHOLOGICAL STUDY OF POLICY DECISIONS AND FIASCOES (2d ed. 1982).
3. Baumeister & Leary, *supra* note 1.
4. Asch, *supra* note 2.
5. Anita Jones Thomas et al, *Racial Identity and Race-Related Stress of African American Parents,* 18 FAMILY J.: COUNSELING AND THERAPY FOR COUPLES AND FAMILIES 407–12 (2010).
6. Hazel Markus & Shinobu Kitayama, *Culture and the Self: Implications for Cognition, Emotion, and Motivation,* 98 PSYCHOL. REV. 224 (1991).
7. *Id.*

presence. On the other hand, we tend to be uneasy around people who are "different" because we don't know what to expect from them. We're uncertain about how to deal with them—and how they may deal with us.

Cultural norms have a powerful unconscious influence on juror decision-making. Jurors intuitively recognize violations of their moral or cultural norms, which have been instilled in them since birth; indeed, these norms may have a greater influence on juror decision-making than the applicable law. This chapter focuses on some of the moral and cultural norms that jurors are likely to rely on, either consciously or unconsciously, when making decisions in our case.[8] These norms, also known as **normative biases**, are primarily Level III decision-making tools, just like those in the last two chapters.

II. Individualistic and Collectivist Cultures

Much psychological and anthropological research has focused on the differences between **individualist and collectivist cultures**.[9] American culture is highly individualistic. We tend to emphasize the importance of the individual and undervalue the importance of group cooperation, i.e., we tend to value independence more than interdependence.[10] Individual achievement, high self-esteem, and personal responsibility have become core American cultural values.

Collectivist cultures, on the other hand, value interdependence and cooperation over individual achievement. For example, people from Far Eastern cultures see themselves as tightly interconnected with a group. They tend to be more cooperative than competitive and are willing to sublimate their desire for individual achievement to advance the fortunes of society as a whole. They value modesty and try to downplay their individual contributions to the group's success.[11]

Because others within our particular culture or subculture share many of the same core values and beliefs, we often fail to appreciate the powerful and pervasive influence that cultural norms have on our thinking and behavior. We are "[l]ike fish unaware of the water in which they are immersed."[12] In other words, we tend to *expect* everyone to think and act like we do. When they don't, we're likely to perceive them as "odd" or "different," which we may unwittingly equate with "abnormal" or "bad."

---

8. *See generally* Daniel L. Schacter, *Implicit Memory: History and Current Status*, 13 J. EXPERIMENTAL PSYCHOL.: LEARNING, MEMORY & COGNITION 501 (1987). Note that many of these cultural biases are commonly shared by other Western European cultures.
9. Richard E. Nisbett & Takahiko Masuda, *Culture and Point of View*, 153 INTELLECTICA 416–47 (2007).
10. CLOTAIRE RAPAILLE, THE CULTURE CODE 173 (2006).
11. Markus & Kitayama, *supra* note 6.
12. DOUGLAS A. BERNSTEIN ET AL., PSYCHOLOGY 24 (8th ed. 2008).

III. Normative Bias

Anyone who has parented a teenager knows the typical justification for misconduct: "Well, everybody else does it!" The implication is clear—if everybody else does it, then it must be acceptable and "normal" behavior. Surely they can't all be wrong.

All of us tend to view our own behavior and that of others like us as the norm, even though it may be well outside of what most people consider to be "normal." This is due to a combination of self-serving biases and cultural norms. The more we think a particular behavior is the same as ours would have been in a similar situation (or what others like us would *expect* it to be), the more "normal" it seems to us, despite what more objective observers might think.

A. Examples of Conforming Conduct to the "Norm"

The normative bias is a powerful motivator. People will go to ridiculous lengths to fit in and be "normal."[13] An interesting and amusing example comes from an old television show called "Candid Camera." The show used actors to put unknowing participants in humorous situations to see how they would react. In one episode, several actors were sitting in a physician's waiting room in their underwear, all behaving normally. Two new patients walked into the room fully clothed. They looked around nervously and sat down. After a short time, they, too, stripped down to their underwear like everyone else. No one had told them to undress—they simply felt compelled to conform to what they perceived to be the applicable norm.

Similarly, in an actual psychological study, a very easy perceptual test was administered. Seven "confederates" (accomplices working with the experimenter) in the room gave a patently wrong answer to a simple question. Despite knowing the correct answer, the eighth person went along with the group's incorrect answer because it didn't seem normal for him to be right and everyone else to be wrong; therefore, he decided not to voice a dissenting opinion for fear that others would view it as outside the norm.[14]

B. The Normative Bias at Trial

The normative bias is pervasive at trial; in fact, the legal standard of care in a civil case is based on societal and professional norms. The law of negligence essentially codifies what "normal" behavior should be by defining "negligence" as the failure to behave as the average, reasonably prudent person

---

13.   John Morreall, Human Works 98 (1997).
14.   Solomon E. Asch, *Effects of Group Pressure Upon the Modification and Distortion of Judgment, in* Groups, Leadership, and Men (Harold Guetzkow, ed. 1951); *see also* Solomon E. Asch, *Opinions and Social Pressure*, 193 Sci. Am. 31–35 (1955).

would in the same or similar situations. In other words, negligence is behavior that falls outside the range of what most people consider to be "normal" and "reasonable" conduct.

Jurors evaluate the conduct of the parties by automatically applying the same normative standards to the evidence that they rely on in everyday life, because these are the only real measuring tools they have.[15] They look for norms or predictable patterns of behavior when deciding fault. If jurors view the conduct in question as "normal," they will probably accept it, particularly if they believe that they would have behaved the same way. Conduct that deviates from the jurors' personal norms, however, is likely to be considered inappropriate.

Long before trial, we must ask ourselves what relevant normative beliefs jurors may have about the parties and the case. We need to answer simple questions like these: What "normally happens," given these particular facts? How do such events "usually" unfold in everyday life? How would the "average" person behave in similar situations? We must also be mindful that our answers to these questions won't be the same as the jurors' answers.

All of us have normative biases, but they vary from person to person and situation to situation. For example, if a police officer is cruising through a "bad" neighborhood at night and he sees a group of young men standing on a street corner, his normative bias may tell him there's a drug deal in progress. But residents of the neighborhood may see the same thing and think nothing of it. Similarly, one parent's "norm" for when to seek medical treatment for a sick child may be "when she's too sick to play with her friends." Another parent may have a very different norm that she applies in the same situation: "whenever I can afford it."

We need to know what information jurors are likely to generalize, distort, or disregard because it's contrary to their beliefs and life experiences. These norms have a profound effect on how jurors are likely to formulate their trial stories because they fill gaps in the story with personal meaning culled from their beliefs, biases, and life experiences.

Conducting focus groups can help us identify the jurors' case-specific norms. Often, focus group participants don't even mention facts that we think are important. We should use this research to guide our fact investigation and discovery. Since many cases don't justify this sort of an investment, it's helpful to know what the more common normative beliefs and biases are that jurors tend to rely on in civil cases. These "juror norms" are described below.

---

15. SUSAN T. FISKE & SHELLEY E. TAYLOR, SOCIAL COGNITION (2d ed. 1991).

1. The Need for Certainty Norm

Jurors like to feel relatively certain about the decisions they make in court and in life. This is why they tend to feel more comfortable making decisions in criminal cases rather than civil cases. The criminal burden of proof requires near-certainty, which is an innately more appealing basis for decision-making than a mere preponderance of the evidence. Requiring proof "beyond a reasonable doubt" seems more fair than simply deciding what's "more likely than not." No one likes to make important decisions that are just a little bit more than half right.

The preponderance of evidence standard is something many jurors aren't familiar with. If they misunderstand the civil burden of proof, however, they'll be reluctant to admit it in open court. If we represent the defendant, we don't need to discuss the burden of proof since confusion is likely to benefit our client. (The exception is having a critical affirmative defense to prove.) But if we represent the plaintiff, we must try to identify those jurors who may be inclined to demand more proof than the law requires. Unfortunately, that's probably the majority of them. So what do we do?

First, we should help jurors understand exactly what "preponderance of the evidence" really means by putting it in context. Attorney Jim Lees of Charleston, West Virginia, suggests asking the following questions during voir dire to accomplish this:

> Q: The plaintiff has the burden of proving her claim in this case. How certain would you need to be before you could decide in favor of the plaintiff?
>
> A: Very certain. I'd want to be pretty darned sure before I made up my mind.
>
> Q: What if I asked you nicely to vote for my client if you were only 70 percent certain. Could you do that?
>
> A: No, no way.
>
> Q: If both the defense attorney and I asked you nicely to vote for the plaintiff if you were only 70 percent certain, could you do it then?
>
> A: Nope.
>
> Q: And even if the judge told you to vote for the plaintiff if you were only 70 percent certain, you, you still couldn't do it, could you?
>
> A: No.

This or a similar series of questions should be asked of jurors we've already identified as probable strikes. To develop a valid challenge for cause, our last question should be a leading question rather than an open-ended one—it's always better to strike jurors for cause than needlessly waste a peremptory challenge.

During closing argument, we should remind jurors of the questions we asked during voir dire to be sure they adhere to the civil burden of proof:

> When you go back to the jury room to decide this case, one of your fellow jurors is probably going to say something like "I'm really not sure." Don't just sit there and be quiet. You have to speak up and remind her that she doesn't *have* to be sure—because certainty is not required in a civil case.

As counsel for the plaintiff, we can't allow jurors to talk about the case in terms of being sure or unsure, so we must remind them that it isn't permitted. We should also add that we're going to prove our case by *more than* a preponderance of the evidence, even though we're not required to. And then, we should do exactly that.

We should assume that most jurors will demand more proof than the law requires because certainty in decision-making is a strong normative bias. This means we must not only prove the defendant was negligent, we must also prove our client was *not* negligent since juror norms are likely to prevail in the jury room, regardless of the law.

2. The Need for Intent Norm

Some jurors may have difficulty understanding why a civil defendant should be "punished" for something he didn't *intend* to do. They may find it difficult to hold someone financially accountable for a mere "accident," even though intent to harm is not required in a civil case.

If we represent a civil defendant, this unspoken need for evidence of intent inures to our benefit. But if we represent an injured plaintiff, we need to spend time explaining how someone can be held accountable for unintentional harm at the beginning of trial.

For example, attorney Jim Lees of Charleston, West Virginia, asks the following questions of the panel during voir dire:

> Q: What do we as a society do with a fellow citizen who intentionally harms another person? Can anyone tell me? Ms. Sanders, you have your hand up. What happens in such cases?

A: We charge that person with a crime, and if they're found guilty, we put them in jail.

Q: So if you were to intentionally harm another human being, you'd be charged with a crime?

A: You betcha.

Q: And you'd be tried in a *criminal* court?

A: Yes. Hurting somebody on purpose is a crime.

Q: So what happens if you *unintentionally* harm someone else? If you have no intention of causing harm to another person, does that mean you still have to go to criminal court?

A: No, I don't think so. Actually, I'm not sure.

Q: Well, let me ask the question this way. Why do some cases go to criminal court and others go to civil court? Does anybody know?

A: We take people to criminal court if they intend to hurt someone—if they know what they're doing and their actions could seriously injure or even kill another person.

Q: But where do cases go when the harm is unintentional—when a person didn't mean to hurt anybody else, but he did?

A: I guess he goes to civil court?

Q: So the difference between criminal court and civil court is whether or not the harm was intentional?

A: Yeah, that's it. If I intend to hurt you, I've committed a crime; but if I hurt you by accident—if I don't mean to hurt you—then I go to civil court.

Q: So all of us agree that if we intentionally harm someone, we can be charged with a crime, and if we're found guilty, we could possibly be sent to prison. But what is the remedy for unintentional harm?

A: Paying somebody money instead of going to jail.

Q: Are you saying you might have to pay money to the person you hurt, even though you didn't intend to hurt her?

A: Yes, I believe so.

Most jurors have never stopped to really think about the difference between the civil and criminal justice systems. Simply telling jurors that a civil case doesn't require intent to harm isn't enough. They need to fully understand and appreciate that a person can be held responsible for the harm he caused, even without intent to harm.

Asking questions similar to the ones above helps jurors better understand how our civil justice system works. It also makes them more likely to apply the burden of proof correctly because they've come to understand it on their own (with a little help from us, of course).

In a medical negligence case, for example, some jurors may want to hear evidence of intent to harm before finding the defendant doctor negligent. These jurors are great for the defense; but if we represent the plaintiff, we must strike them because they will refuse to find the defendant liable unless we can prove intent to harm. As long as they believe the defendant doctor used his best medical judgment in treating his patient, "He didn't mean to do it" is reason enough for many of them to deny relief to our client.

Therefore, if we represent the plaintiff, it's essential for us to specifically ask jurors if they'll be willing to compensate our client for the harm she suffered if we can prove our case. For example:

Q: This is a civil medical negligence case that involves unintentional harm. We're not alleging that Dr. Manning *intended* to harm Ms. Lasko. If he had intended to harm her, he could be charged with a crime and tried in criminal court rather than civil court. Does everyone understand that if Dr. Manning intended to harm Ms. Lasko, this would be a criminal case? If so, please raise your hand.

A: [Jurors raise their hands.]

Q: Because we're in civil court, I need to know if anyone has a problem with compensating a patient for injuries she has suffered because the doctor *unintentionally* harmed her?

A: Yes, I do. We shouldn't hold doctors responsible for unintended results. It's not fair to make a doctor pay for something he didn't mean to do.

Q: So even if the judge tells you that the law allows an injured patient to be compensated for the harm she suffered, you couldn't do that in this case?

Once we find jurors who are likely to demand proof of intent to harm, we should strike them for cause, if possible. Failing that, we should strike them with a peremptory challenge because they will demand more proof than the law requires and may convince others to do likewise during deliberations.

3. The Status Quo Norm

People are naturally inclined to preserve the status quo. (*See* discussion of the status quo in chapter eight, section II(C)(2).) Change is frightening. We fear the unknown because we can't predict how it will affect us; therefore, we feel uncertain and unsafe.

When jurors are uncertain of the right decision—when they believe the evidence doesn't clearly favor one side or the other—they prefer to leave things as they are. But the status quo to jurors is the way things are when the trial begins. To the injured plaintiff, however, the status quo is life as it was before she was injured.

Although maintaining the status quo favors the defense, it doesn't do the same for the plaintiff. She needs jurors to take affirmative action to change the status quo.

When we combine the jurors' need for certainty with their decided preference for the status quo, we can see that the injured plaintiff is at a distinct disadvantage from the outset. But jurors are reluctant to act unless they feel fairly certain the defendant is responsible for the outcome. Otherwise, they prefer to leave things as they are.

4. The "Politically Correct" Norm

Jurors feel compelled to comply with what they perceive as relevant societal and cultural norms. During voir dire, for example, it can be difficult to elicit honest answers from jurors who feel that a truthful answer will be viewed as socially unacceptable. Like all human beings, jurors are willing to color the truth rather than voice socially unacceptable opinions in public. They "go along to get along." Although their reluctance to be honest with us is understandable, what jurors *fail* to tell us are often the things that are most important for us to know.

To fully explore potential juror biases, we need to make each juror feel comfortable about confessing any biases they may have. Phrasing difficult questions in the alternative and letting jurors choose between two opposing points of view helps "normalize" both viewpoints, without suggesting that one is more acceptable than another. Consider this example:

> I understand that some of you might have strong feelings about people who bring claims for their injuries to court. For example, some jurors may worry that a verdict for the plaintiff might

cause their insurance premiums to rise. Others may believe that insurance companies make money by denying valid claims and charging higher premiums than necessary. *Which viewpoint are you a little closer to?*

Offering opposing alternatives makes it easier for jurors to articulate their beliefs and biases. It also makes it easier for us to identify those jurors who simply cannot be fair, no matter what the evidence may be.

If we're able to elicit a potential bias, we should probe further and try to develop a challenge for cause:

> How long have you held this viewpoint? Do you feel strongly about it? What would it take to change your mind? Other than that, what else could change your mind? Would you ever really change your mind just because you were told to do so? If you said "yes" to the person who was asking you to change your mind, would you agree just to be polite?

Answers to these questions can help us develop more effective challenges for cause.

5. The Aversion to Loss Norm

Interestingly, people are more motivated to avoid a potential loss than to realize an equivalent potential gain. In civil cases, some jurors may believe that a verdict for the plaintiff is ultimately going to be a loss to them. They imagine that if the plaintiff "gains" money from the lawsuit, they will suffer a commensurate "loss" in the form of increased prices for insurance, goods, and services when the costs of litigation are "passed on to the poor consumer."

Jurors understand that the criminal justice system is designed to protect them; but few are aware that the civil justice system does the same thing. If we represent the plaintiff, we must be careful to frame our case in a way that helps jurors understand that a verdict for the defendant could ultimately result in a loss for them and their community by making it less safe.

Jurors will inevitably ask themselves: If we find for the plaintiff, will the defendant automobile manufacturer really try to make our cars safer? Or will they simply raise the price of their cars (which is a loss to *me*)? Will a verdict for the plaintiff in a medical malpractice make *me* safer by causing doctors to be more careful? Or will it cause the defendant doctor (and other doctors) to move to elsewhere to practice medicine, resulting in a shortage of available medical care?

As lawyers, we must tread a fine line. The Golden Rule prevents us from making personal appeals to jurors; but if we represent the plaintiff, we also don't want jurors to fear they'll become the ultimate victims of their own verdict if they award sizeable damages to the plaintiff. We all make decisions in our own self-interest—even when the decision they're making isn't about *us*. This is an automatic Level I response because the need to maintain the status quo—our current level of safety—is a basic survival response. Unfortunately, like so many other biases, it tends to disfavor the plaintiff.

"Rules" and powerful themes are the best ways to help jurors understand that the defendant's actions had the potential to harm *anyone*. But we must not add, "Including *you*." They need to understand that justice for our client is not injustice for them, but maintaining and increasing the level of safety for everyone.

IV. "Imprinting" and "Culture Codes"

"Imprinting" is the process by which young animals learn appropriate or "normal" behavior from their parents by instinctively mimicking it. For example, young goslings "imprint" on the mother goose and learn to follow her wherever she goes—a critical skill since they're unable to protect themselves from harm.[16] (Interestingly, biologist Konrad Lorenz discovered that goslings hatched in an incubator actually imprinted on him and began to follow him around as if they were his offspring.[17])

Some psychologists believe that imprinting occurs in humans as well as animals. Clinical psychologist Alfred Adler noted that his patients' earliest memories of a particular experience seemed to be the most important, particularly if the experience was a highly emotional one.[18] Such experiences form indelible "imprints" in our minds. Later, they become the starting point for how we think about similar experiences and how we view ourselves in relation to those experiences.

Adler theorized that imprints condition us to think about certain things in a certain way for the rest of our lives.[19] Even today, psychologists and psychiatrists may occasionally focus on our earliest memories and emotions because they have such a significant effect on our lives. Some experts believe that we're born with certain "innate imprints" (similar to Carl Jung's theory

---

16. Julian Jaynes, *Imprinting: The Interaction of Learned and Innate Behavior,* 49 J. Comp. & Physiological Psychol. 201–06 (1956); Barbara S. Kisilevsky, *Effects of Experience on Fetal Voice Recognition,* 14(3) Psychol. Sci. 220–24 (2003).
17. Konrad Lorenz, King Solomon's Ring (Marjorie Kerr Wilson trans., 1961).
18. Alfred Adler, The Practice and Theory of Individual Psychology (1963). Adler's original work was published in 1927, so these theories have been around for quite some time.
19. *Id.*

of the **collective unconscious**) because there are things we simply "know" without having to learn.[20]

In his provocative book, *The Culture Code*, Clotaire Rapaille, a French-born child psychologist and cultural anthropologist, also propounds the notion that people "imprint" in much the same way that animals do.[21] Rapaille, like Adler, argues that we make indelible imprints in our brains during early childhood whenever we experience something for the first time. These imprints create mental connections or neural pathways that we automatically rely on to make decisions for the rest of our lives.[22] The stronger the emotions connected with the initial imprint, the more profound its effect on our future thoughts and actions.[23]

The meaning that we ascribe to these imprints is, to a large extent, culturally dependent. Most of us spend a great deal of time at home during our formative years when most imprinting occurs (from birth to age seven).[24] Because people are generally exposed to only one culture during early childhood, people from different cultures tend to react quite differently to the same things.[25]

For example, French children are not prohibited from drinking wine. They learn to enjoy it for its flavor and how it enhances food at an early age. American children generally take their first drink as teenagers, often with the intent to get drunk. Consequently, French children and American children form very different imprints of alcohol.[26] Rather than viewing alcohol as an enjoyable complement to a good meal, American teenagers tend to connect alcohol with an illicit sort of excitement.[27]

Rapaille believes these initial imprints are the key to what he calls **culture codes**: "The culture code is the unconscious meaning we apply to any given thing—a car, a type of food, a relationship, even a country—via the culture in which we are raised."[28] Culture codes lead people from different cultures to process the same information in different ways.[29]

---

20. More popular cognitive behavioral therapies focus more on the present and future rather than the past, which was typical of the older psychoanalytic approach. *See, e.g.,* B.R. Hergenhahn & M. Olson, Introduction to Theories of Personality (7th ed. 2007) (discussing Carl Jung's theory of the **collective unconscious** or memories we inherited from human and animal ancestors).

21. Clotaire Rapaille, The Culture Code 5–6 (2006). Rapaille studied under the famous childhood development psychologist, Jean Piaget.

22. *Id.* at 17.

23. *Id.*

24. *Id.* at 21.

25. *Id.* at 26–27.

26. *Id.* at 23.

27. *Id.* at 151–53.

28. *Id.* at 5.

29. *Id.* at 5–6.

Rapaille's research focuses on how our earliest childhood memories of something "imprint" strong preferences in our minds—preferences that can predict how consumers in a particular market will respond to a certain product. Rapaille has been immensely successful at devising marketing strategies based on this research. By marketing products in a way that appeals to consumer culture codes, he has become him one of the most successful marketing consultants and political advisors in the world.[30]

Although Rapaille's methods are somewhat controversial,[31] his theories provide interesting insights into automatic decision-making. If these theories are correct, Rapaille's culture codes may also affect juror decision-making.[32]

A. The Culture Code

Rapaille subscribes to the **triune brain theory**, which postulates that the human brain is separated into three distinct parts.[33] The first is the cortex or cognitive part of our brain: the thinking center that gives us the ability to reason.[34] The second is the limbic system, the seat of our emotions; and the third is the **reptilian brain**, the most basic and primitive part of our brain that controls our fundamental instinct to survive and reproduce.[35] (*Note that neither the term "reptilian brain" nor triune brain theory is generally accepted in psychological literature.*[36])

Rapaille believes that the cortex is more concerned with impression management than truth-telling. All of us "manage" our appearances and try to

---

30. Rapaille is on retainer to fifty Fortune 100 companies and serves as a personal advisor to ten high-ranking CEOs. *Id.* at 11. He also served as an advisor to George W. Bush's presidential campaign. He encouraged Bush operatives to focus on non-political issues like religion and abortion rather than specific social or economic issues to win the election. *Id.* at 184.

31. Rapaille conducts "discovery sessions" or marketing research to find out how participants initially imprinted a particular product. In the first hour of these sessions, Rapaille pretends to be a visitor from another planet who has never seen or experienced the product before. Participants are asked to help this "space visitor" understand the product by sharing their thoughts about it. In the second hour, participants sit on the floor like young school children and cut out words from magazines to make a collage of the product that tells a story about it. In the third hour, participants go into a darkened room, lie on the floor on pillows, listen to soothing music, and then answer questions about their earliest memories of a particular thing or experience by accessing their "reptilian brains." *Id.* at 8, 15.

32. *See also* Kathryn A. Broun-LaTour et al, *Using Childhood Memories to Gain Insight into Brand Meaning,* 71 J. OF MARKETING 45–60 (Apr. 2007).

33. Rapaille's theories are based on "triune brain theory," which was developed by Paul MacLean. *See* PAUL MACLEAN, A TRIUNE CONCEPT OF THE BRAIN AND BEHAVIOR (1973).

34. Rapaille, *supra* note 21, at 73.

35. *Id.* at 74. This is an overly simplistic concept of the limbic system. For more information on the limbic system, *see* MARK F. BEAR ET AL, NEUROSCIENCE: EXPLORING THE BRAIN (3d ed. 2007).

36. Triune brain theory oversimplifies the evolution of intelligence, which has followed different paths among different groups of animals. *See, e.g.,* Paul Patton, *One World, Many Minds: Intelligence in the Animal Kingdom,* SCI. AM. MIND, Dec. 2008.

present ourselves in a way that will encourage others to like us.[37] We rely on our cortex to filter and censor thought so that we don't speak without thinking and blurt out socially unacceptable truths. According to Rapaille, if we can delve beyond the cortex and limbic systems into the "reptilian brain," we can more accurately discern someone's true thoughts and feelings.[38] He believes that instinct will always prevail over logic and emotion because survival is so fundamental to our existence.[39]

Rapaille asserts that the "reptilian brain" is the key to identifying culture codes.[40] If we can appeal to a person's "reptilian brain," which controls our most basic (and often *basest*) instincts, Rapaille believes that we can elicit predictable, automatic responses.[41] Because each culture has its own unique and distinctive cultural mindset, Rapaille searches for a one- or two-word archetype or "culture code" that captures the essence of a particular society's "collective cultural unconscious" about an idea or thing. These simple codes are metaphors or themes that reveal the fundamental nature of a particular culture and how its people think and behave.[42]

For example, Rapaille believes the American culture code for "doctor" is "hero," and the code for nurse is "mother" or "caretaker."[43] Interestingly, however, the code for "hospital" is "factory" or "processing plant."[44] Hospitals are big, impersonal places filled with strange equipment (machinery) where our movement is constrained and we're relegated to our beds.[45] (A scary thought for those of us who represent hospitals and their administrators.)

B. Culture Codes in the Marketplace

In the late 1990s, the Chrysler Corporation hired Rapaille to market the Jeep Wrangler, which had lost its popularity in the American market. Wrangler's market share had been eroded by a host of bigger, more comfortable SUVs, so Chrysler hired Rapaille to fix the problem.[46]

Rapaille began by researching American culture codes. He discovered that we're an "adolescent" culture with a youthful, action-oriented approach to life that is markedly different from the older, "grayer" cultures of Europe

---

37. Michael E. Sadler et al, *Personality and Impression Management: Mapping the Multidimensional Personality Questionnaire onto 12 Self-Presentation Tactics,* 48 PERSONALITY AND INDIVIDUAL DIFFERENCES 623–28 (2010).
38. RAPAILLE, *supra* note 21, at 73–74.
39. *Id.* at 74.
40. *Id.* at 5, 10–11.
41. *Id.* at 74.
42. *Id.* at 10–11, 27–28.
43. *Id.* at 82.
44. *Id.* at 83.
45. *Id.*
46. *Id.* at 1.

where Rapaille was reared.[47] He saw our culture as one that thrives on fast food, loud music, "action heroes," energy drinks, running shoes, and violent movies, so he devised a marketing campaign that incorporated "the trappings of adolescence"—one that would appeal to our fiercely independent, young, and restless culture.[48]

Rapaille used a uniquely American iconic image to sell Jeep Wranglers in this country: that of brave pioneers heading west to conquer new and uncharted territory on horseback. He created a television ad for Jeep that shows a young boy hiking in the mountains with his dog. The dog suddenly falls off a cliff and is clinging precariously to a tree. The distraught boy runs to a nearby village for help, passing sedans, minivans, SUVs, and finally, a Jeep Wrangler. The driver of the Wrangler scales the mountain, rescues the dog, and heads off into the sunset before the boy can thank him.[49] The "reptilian" message was that this is a real American tough guy riding away on his "horse" (Rapaille's culture code for "Jeep") to confront and conquer the next challenge looming on the horizon.[50] (The Jeep campaign is reminiscent of the popular "Marlboro man" ads of the sixties and seventies that featured a rugged-looking cowboy riding a horse on the wide-open plains and smoking a cigarette.)

This "on code" message was very successful in America; however, Rapaille knew that he had to devise a different marketing strategy for the Jeep Wrangler in France. He discovered that the French culture code for "Jeep" was "liberator." The French associated Wranglers with the Jeeps driven into France by American soldiers at the close of World War II to liberate their country from Nazi rule. Accordingly, Rapaille designed a French campaign that "stressed the Jeep's proud past and the freedom gained from driving a Wrangler."[51]

C. American Culture Codes at Trial

Rapaille's research revealed a variety of self-serving biases that are deeply ingrained in American culture. For example, we strongly believe in the notion of a just world and the illusion of control. The stereotypical "American dream" is to be a "good" person who works hard and is richly rewarded for his efforts.[52] Imbedded within this dream is the belief that we have the ability to control potential outcomes in life and that good conduct will always be rewarded. We're convinced that we can make it on our own if we try

---

47. *Id.* at 33–34.
48. *Id.* at 31.
49. *Id.* at 3.
50. *Id.* at 2.
51. *Id.* at 3.
52. Rapaille believes that the culture code for America is "dream." *Id.* at 195.

hard enough, and so can anyone else. We pride ourselves on being strong, independent, self-sufficient people, even though that may not always be an entirely accurate self-portrait.

As a "culturally adolescent" society, we see ourselves as eternally young, strong, and invincible—traits that have served us well in the long run.[53] But our obsession with staying young and strong also makes us impatient, quick to find fault or assign blame, and often prejudiced against those who are less fortunate than we.

Our attributional biases make us prone to claim credit for our own successes, yet equally prone to hold others personally accountable for whatever *bad* things may happen to them. In the courtroom, these biases, when coupled American individualism, tend to generate a palpable prejudice against plaintiffs and criminal defendants. It's as though jurors are programmed to view them as people who weren't "tough" enough to play by the rules and make it on their own—people who must look elsewhere for help because they're unable to fend for themselves. This biased perception is difficult for a plaintiff or criminal defendant to overcome.

Arguably, we can implement some of Rapaille's theories (if not his techniques) at trial. If we can appeal to jurors on a primal, culturally mandated level, we may be able to convince them to act on that level, thereby eliciting predictable responses. To that end, we will discuss some of the strongest American "cultural biases," which presumably exist at a primal, subconscious level, and explore their effects on modern jurors.

1. Personal Responsibility

More than 95 percent of Americans rank the concept of personal responsibility as one of the most important values in our society.[54] This belief remains consistent across gender, race, class, and political preference.[55] More than 80 percent of us consider ourselves to be more responsible than others, better able to make wise decisions, and better judges of character.[56]

What is this about? At the base of Maslow's hierarchical pyramid of needs (*see* chapter three) is insuring our own survival and that of our family. To achieve this goal, we have to believe that we are capable of affecting the outcome in any situation by applying sound judgment and hard work. At its core, personal responsibility is the belief that anyone who is hurt or anyone

---

53. *Id.* at 85.
54. David A. Wenner & Gregory S. Cusimano, *Combating Juror Bias*, TRIAL 30 (June 2000).
55. *Id.*
56. Douglas L. Keene & Paul Begala, *The Jury Project, Part I: Juror Attitudes and Biases,* Keene Trial Consulting, at 13–14, *available at* www.keenetrial.com.

who has "allowed" a family member to be hurt must have failed to protect himself or his loved ones.

The mantra of "personal responsibility" resonates with us because the belief in a just world and the illusion of control are very strong in individualistic cultures.[57] As a result, jurors may initially be inclined to deny relief to the plaintiff. They secretly suspect that she *must* have done something wrong—something she's unwilling to accept responsibility for—since she suffered such a bad outcome.[58] The concept of personal responsibility has another unfortunate consequence: it may lead jurors to hold the plaintiff to a higher standard of proof than the law requires.

Not surprisingly, personal responsibility is often used to great advantage by the defense in civil cases. As we have seen, jurors automatically rely on defensive attribution to distance themselves from an injured plaintiff because they're reluctant to identify with someone who has been badly hurt. Doing so would be tantamount to admitting that the same thing could happen to them, a sentiment that has generated palpable prejudice against plaintiffs in American courtrooms.

Some jurors view lawsuits as little more than a plaintiff's attempt to shift responsibility for the consequences of her own actions or inaction to someone or something else. As plaintiff's counsel, we must be prepared to deal with these jurors and their inclination to hold our client accountable for the harm she suffered. Their overwhelming need to feel safe, coupled with the powerful cultural norm of "personal responsibility," makes it difficult for us to prove to these jurors that the plaintiff was an innocent victim of someone else's wrongdoing or negligence.

Despite this, plaintiff's counsel can turn the tables and use the concept of personal responsibility to show that the defendant failed to accept personal responsibility for the harm that he caused. This is a particularly effective tactic if our client has valiantly struggled to overcome the ill effects of her injury. If jurors are convinced the plaintiff has done everything possible to mitigate the harm she has suffered, they may choose to award damages on the theory that the money will be well-spent on someone who has demonstrated personal responsibility and done everything possible to overcome adversity.

Exceptional misconduct provides the plaintiff with yet another avenue of recovery. Jurors are understandably more willing to punish *exceptional* mis-

---

57.   Harmon M. Hosch,, *A Comparison of Anglo-American & Mexican American Jurors' Judgments of Mothers Who Fail to Protect their Children from Abuse*, 21 J. APPLIED SOC. PSYCHOL. 1681–98 (1991).

58.   For an explanation of this "blame the victim" propensity and its causes, *see* Kees van den Bos & Marjolein Maas, *On the Psychology of the Belief in a Just World: Explaining Experimental and Rationalistic Paths to Victim-Blaming*, 35 PERSONALITY & SOC. PSYCHOL. BULL. 1567–78 (2009).

conduct—conduct unlikely to recur—because they can hold the defendant responsible without feeling personally threatened by what happened. If we can highlight many instances in which the defendant behaved irresponsibly, we may be able to make a case for "exceptional" rather than "ordinary" negligence.

2. Suspicion of Lawyers and the Civil Justice System

Jurors, like all human beings, are naturally suspicious creatures.[59] Some degree of suspicion is healthy and protective. We're inherently suspicious of people and things we don't know or understand because they may pose a potential threat to our safety; therefore, we're naturally suspicious of everyone and everything that makes us afraid.

Unfortunately, most jurors are suspicious of lawyers because we're relatively unknown quantities to them. The majority of them have limited personal experience with lawyers, the law, and the legal process. Much of what they've heard and read about our profession is negative. Consequently, they're not inclined to regard us as reliable sources of information, particularly since they know we're being paid to take a side. Because people intuitively interpret any message in light of the messenger's personal credibility, it may be difficult for us to earn the jurors' trust and respect.[60]

The strident rhetoric of tort reform has only heightened juror suspicions about us and the entire civil justice system, particularly the validity of claims made by injured plaintiffs.[61] Their suspicions will be heightened even further when the facts of our case make them fear for their own safety or that of loved ones—a problem every personal injury plaintiff must face.

---

59.   William J. McGuire, *Inducing Resistance to Persuasion: Some Contemporary Approaches*, *in* 1 ADVANCES IN EXPERIMENTAL SOCIAL PSYCHOLOGY, 191 (1964).

60.   Some commentators have asserted that nearly half of our jurors are likely to believe that we'll say whatever it takes to win, with little regard for truth. *See, e.g.,* Larry S. Miller, *Jury Reform: An Analysis of Juror Perceptions of the Criminal Court System*, 10 CRIM. JUST. REV. 11 (1985).

61.   *See, e.g.,* David M. Studdert et al., *Claims, Errors, and Compensation Payments in Medical Malpractice Litigation*, 354 NEW ENG. J. MED. 2024 (2006). Researchers at the Harvard School of Public Health conducted a study of the medical errors, costs, and claims of 1,452 medical malpractice lawsuits. Each case was reviewed by independent medical professionals to determine whether, in their opinion, a medical error had been committed. They then compared their findings to the actual outcomes at trial.

Looking at the 208 cases that were tried, independent medical professionals found ninety-one cases of medical error, or 44 percent. Jury verdicts were rendered for the plaintiff in fifty of those ninety-one cases, i.e., in only 24 percent of all cases tried. The researchers found medical errors in forty-one cases in which the plaintiff recovered nothing.

The average time from injury to settlement or verdict was five years, with one in three claims taking six years or more to resolve. While awaiting an outcome, plaintiffs obviously bore the costs and burdens that flowed from these medical errors.

Some jurors may be inclined to deny relief to the plaintiff because they see *themselves* as potential victims of unscrupulous plaintiffs who try to recover damages they don't deserve. These jurors believe that frivolous lawsuits and outrageous damage awards have unfairly increased the cost of their insurance premiums as well as other goods and services or have forced them to take actions they don't like, such as implementing expensive or time-consuming safety procedures in their business or workplace. This may make jurors more reluctant to award compensation to the plaintiff for fear that the direct or indirect costs of litigation will be passed on to them as consumers. Because these jurors think of themselves as surrogate stakeholders in the case, they're more inclined to deny relief to the plaintiff for reasons unrelated to the merits of her case.[62]

Some jurors will simply refuse to find in favor of the plaintiff, regardless of the facts of the case. Our job is to try to identify these jurors during voir dire and strike them, because efforts to change their normative biases and personal philosophy will be futile.

3. Stereotyping and the Ultimate Attribution Error

Our cultural biases may cause us to develop prototypes or **schemas** (discussed in chapter two) that we automatically use to draw inferences and conclusions about unfamiliar people, things, or events, often unfairly or inaccurately. Over time, we may begin to develop **positive and negative stereotypes** that we rely on to guide our future behavior.[63]

A variety of self-serving biases incline us to see ourselves as a composite of many different talents and abilities; however, we tend *not to* attribute such qualities to other people, particularly if they're considerably different from us. We tend to view "strangers" as one-dimensional people who are similar to one another, but dissimilar to us, merely because we lack sufficient context to judge those we know the least about. This tendency may cause us to make unfair generalizations about people from other cultures or backgrounds, based either on ignorance or a few isolated personal experiences.

This sort of negative stereotyping is often referred to as the **ultimate attribution error** because it can lead us to "attribute" certain personal characteristics or personality traits to an entire group rather than an individual.[64] For example, some people believe that politicians (or lawyers) can't be trusted, that Muslims are affiliated with terrorist organizations, or that men are better

---

62.   *See generally* Wenner & Cusimano, *supra* note 54.
63.   Bernstein, *supra* note 12, at 707–08.
64.   Thomas Pettigrew, *The Ultimate Attribution Error: Extending Allport's Cognitive Analysis of Prejudice,* 5 Personality & Soc. Psychol. Bull. 461–76 (1979).

drivers than women. In each case, there is an example that can be cited for the proposition, but the generalization from the example is inaccurate.

If these cultural biases or stereotypes are widely subscribed to by jurors' families, friends, or social, ethnic, or religious groups, jurors may be unaware of these biases, believing their view of the world is accurate. Even if they do recognize their biases, they may be unwilling to admit having them because they prefer not to be judged for holding views that others find unpopular or unacceptable.

Jurors are not alone in harboring biases. Lawyers and other types of professionals tend to look at things according to the conventions of their chosen profession, often disregarding other viewpoints. We must be careful not to classify a particular case as "just another domestic dispute" lest our diagnosis become a self-fulfilling prophecy.

Stereotyping is no less invidious because it's done by a "professional." It still amounts to squeezing a client's case into an ill-fitting mold, simply because we think "we've seen it before." What we believe is the most plausible explanation for what happened may lead us to make unfounded assumptions based on past professional experience rather than reality.

4. Overcoming Cultural Biases

Personal responsibility has long been a weapon in the civil defense lawyer's arsenal. For example, in the ongoing "tobacco war" cases, counsel for the defendant tobacco companies have made compelling arguments about plaintiffs' conscious decisions to continue smoking cigarettes long after they were aware of the risks:

> After being a smoker for forty-five years, the plaintiff is refusing to take personal responsibility for the consequences of her actions. She knew that smoking was bad for her. She knew it when she started. But that didn't stop her from starting a pack-a-day habit as a teenager. Soon, it became two packs a day. Sometimes, it was three packs a day. No one held a gun to her head and told her she had to smoke—or that she couldn't stop once she started. She made a deliberate, conscious choice to smoke pack after pack, year after year. But now she wants to blame the company that manufactured her cigarettes for her three-pack-a-day habit.

To counteract this argument, plaintiff's counsel can use the personal responsibility argument against the defendant tobacco company and do it *first*:

This company knew that smoking was harmful to your health in the 1950s. Their own in-house researchers knew that smoking cigarettes could kill you. Yet the company concealed this information from the public. It continued to market cigarettes on television, on the radio, in magazines and newspapers, on billboards. It chose to sell a dangerous product to the plaintiff and millions like her who didn't know what the company knew. People who *couldn't* know what the company never told them. And now that company is saying. "Yes, we knew, but we're not responsible for what people do with our highly addictive, deadly product . . . ."

Because people often don't recognize their own biases, particularly those that are widely shared by others in the culture, it's difficult to fault jurors for clinging to their biases, even in the face of evidence that refutes those biases. The only option in some cases is to strike those jurors who are biased in favor of our opponent and to keep those whom we believe will be fair to our client. Sadly, we're often mistaken about who will be a "good" or "bad" juror for our side.

If we learn to identify these biases and others that are specific to our case, preferably well in advance of trial, we can develop facts, theories, themes, and strategies that allow us to link these biases and beliefs to our case. We need to create a trial strategy that will embrace the jury's likely perceptions of the evidence.

If we discover they have strong biases against our client or compelling reasons to find in favor of our opponent, we should try to settle the case. But if we can get jurors to do the right thing, realizing that appeals to reason and logic may not achieve that lofty goal, we can help jurors find other pathways to the same result. We just have to be sure that their unconscious coping strategies, deeply ingrained biases, and life experiences don't pose insurmountable obstacles along the way.

CHAPTER EIGHT

HEURISTICS AND OTHER INFORMATION-PROCESSING STRATEGIES

I. Introduction to Reasoning and Heuristics

Reasoning is the process of generating potential arguments for and against information so we can decide what the information really means and what we should do with it.[1] As trial lawyers, we're accustomed to using **formal or deductive reasoning** in the everyday practice of law. We take general rules and apply them to specific cases in order to reach valid conclusions, a process that requires considerable time and effort. This sort of reasoning is at the top of the hierarchy of decision-making.

For example, we prepare for trial by analyzing and evaluating the facts of a case in light of the applicable law and rules of evidence and procedure. We try to generate every conceivable argument that can be made for and against our position to decide which arguments will be most persuasive to the jury. This is how we arrive at our "theory of the case." Although this type of reasoning isn't foolproof, it generally yields sound conclusions.

Unfortunately, no one can rely on formal reasoning all the time because it's rigorous and time-consuming and it depletes our limited cognitive resources. This is why **informal or inductive reasoning** is indispensable for making simple, routine decisions in our daily lives. Inductive reasoning involves using specific facts or examples of what we already know to figure out and draw conclusions about what we *don't* know—without relying on any formal rules, systematic procedures, or mathematical formulas.

Heuristics are a type of informal reasoning that comprise Level IV of our hierarchy of decision-making. Heuristics are simply mental shortcuts or rules of thumb that we commonly rely on to make decisions. Heuristic processing helps us make decisions quickly and efficiently. It also conserves our precious

---

1. Douglas A. Bernstein et al., Psychology 290–91 (8th ed. 2008); James K. Kuklinski & Paul J. Quirk, *Reconsidering the Rational Public: Cognition, Heuristics, and Mass Opinion, in* Elements of Reason: Cognition, Choice, and the Bounds of Rationality, 153, 155–57 (Arthur Lupia et al. eds., 2000).

cognitive resources and helps alleviate the stress of indecision. When we're not operating at the Levels I or II of our hierarchy of decision-making, we generally opt for Levels III and IV, since these levels of reasoning are quicker and easier than using logic, which is often our course of last resort.

Most heuristics operate automatically, i.e., beyond our level of conscious awareness.[2] Heuristics work well in situations that don't require an optimum result or outcome, because they allow us to make reasonably good decisions with minimal effort. But when we apply heuristic processing inappropriately, it often leads to consistent, predictable mistakes in judgment (**thinking errors**) because we sacrifice accuracy for speed and conceptual simplicity. In other words, we make what psychologists refer to as a **speed-accuracy tradeoff**.[3]

For example, when grocery shopping, we tend to equate a well-known brand name with "high quality." We don't have the time or inclination to do extensive research on everything we buy, so we rely on a heuristic that "brand names are better" to simplify and expedite shopping trips. (Apparently, this particular heuristic is fairly accurate because so much marketing is based on it.) However, the kind of "quick and dirty" decision-making we use for grocery shopping is inherently inappropriate for making the kinds of decisions that we ask jurors to make at trial.

To help jurors reach a just result and avoid the pitfalls of heuristic thinking, we must understand the cognitive tools they use in their everyday lives. These are the same tools they will automatically use to make decisions at trial. For example, a juror in a criminal trial may use the heuristic that "most criminal defendants are probably guilty of something" to conclude the current defendant is guilty. Similarly, a civil juror's heuristic that "lawsuits are only about winning the lawsuit lottery" may lead that juror to conclude the current plaintiff is malingering.

Although heuristic processing may reduce the amount of subjective uncertainty that jurors experience, it can also lead to a miscarriage of justice. Therefore, we have to accept the fact that jurors, like everyone else, generally prefer to stay on Levels I, II, and III of the hierarchy of decision-making because they're cognitive misers. They don't want to mentally exert themselves if they don't have to. Problems that jurors believe will have no personal impact on their lives usually go into the "I don't have to" category, so logic loses out.

---

2. The terms "unconscious" and "subconscious" are infrequently used in psychological literature today. They have been replaced with the term "automatic," which refers to mental processes that occur beyond our level of awareness. "Controlled" mental processes are just the opposite: they are synonymous with conscious thought.
3. Christopher D. Wickens & C. Melody Carswell, *Information Processing, in* Handbook of Human Factors and Ergonomics 111, 134–35 (Gavriel Salvendy ed., 3d ed. 2006).

Fortunately, heuristics operate in predictable patterns. If we understand what these patterns are and how heuristic processing affects juror decision-making, we can structure our evidence to account for the inevitable thinking errors caused by inappropriate use of heuristics.

A. How We Create Heuristics

Heuristics are roughly the cognitive equivalent of "memory scripts" (discussed in chapter two). Heuristics help us *make decisions* automatically, while memory scripts help us *perform physical activities* involving routine, repetitive movements automatically. For example, once we learn how to ride a bike, we no longer have to stop and think about each discrete step in the process such as how to pedal, steer, and stop because we create "memory scripts" for these sorts of activities. We gradually learn how to execute each step of the process so well that biking no longer requires conscious thought. We just do it automatically.

In much the same fashion, certain routine, repetitive cognitive tasks become second nature to us because we've performed them so many times before. We initially create heuristics through a process of trial and error. We repeat our successes and failures in life until we figure out the proper sequence of mental shortcuts that will get us successively closer to a desired result on a regular, reliable basis.[4] Heuristics spare us the burden of constantly "reinventing the wheel" whenever we perform certain routine mental tasks because we don't have to stop and think about what to do next.

So going back to our earlier example in the grocery store, let's presume we buy the brand name and we're satisfied with everything but the price. We resolve to buy the store brand the next time, but when we do, we're disappointed with the quality, so we go back to the brand name. After a while, still unhappy about the higher price, we try the store brand again, hoping it has been improved. But it still disappoints us and back we go to the brand name product. Eventually, we reach the conclusion that brand names are better, so we swear off store brands. Whatever we go to buy, we run our "shopping experience tape" quickly and reach for the brand name without thinking—even when we're not buying groceries. This is how we create heuristics or mental shortcuts over time that help us make decisions automatically, efficiently, and quickly.

Imagine how difficult life must be for people who stop and ponder every step involved in every decision they make. Just watching them order din-

---

4. Jean Piaget, The Origins of Intelligence in Children (1936). Piaget noted that children learn through trial and error. Even infants learn the physical properties of the world through trial and error and will generalize their findings about a physical object to other objects. For example, if a string attached to a toy can be tugged to bring it closer, the same will be true of other toys.

ner in a restaurant is painful. Deciding what to wear must be a tedious and time-consuming ordeal for them. In short, we need heuristics to function efficiently in our daily lives.

B. Why Jurors Rely on Heuristics

Just as we need heuristics in our daily lives, jurors often default to heuristic processing at trial because it helps them process the evidence more quickly and efficiently, even if less accurately. It also relieves information overload and the stress of indecision. We must recognize that not every juror will be willing to invest the requisite time and cognitive effort necessary to achieve the best possible result at trial.

Jurors with a low **need for cognition** (those who don't enjoy cognitive effort) tend to rely on heuristics more often than those who typically enjoy mental stimulation and challenges.[5] (*See* discussion of need for cognition in chapter three.) But even jurors with a high need for cognition will resort to heuristic processing whenever they feel the decision holds little relevance for them.[6]

Because jurors rely on heuristic processing automatically, they're generally unaware of how it may affect their decisions. Nevertheless, inappropriate reliance on heuristics can actually alter or distort the jurors' perceptions of the evidence.[7] Therefore, it falls to us to minimize the potential damage this may cause.

II. Three Primary Heuristics

In 1974, psychologists Amos Tversky and Daniel Kahneman (who won the 2002 Nobel Prize in economics for his work) identified three primary heuristics that people use when making judgments and decisions in their everyday lives: (1) the representativeness heuristic; (2) the availability heuristic; and (3) the anchoring heuristic.[8] A basic understanding of each of these heuristics can help us predict how jurors are likely to react to the evidence presented at trial.

---

5. Note, however, that some research actually suggests that thinking too deeply can also lead to thinking errors. *See* Zakary L. Tormala et al., *Ease of Retrieval Effects in Persuasion: A Self-Validation Analysis,* 28 Personality & Soc. Psychol. Bull. 1700–12 (2002).
6. Michael R. Leipe & Roger A. Elkin, *When Motives Clash: Issue Involvement and Response Involvements as Determinants of Persuasion,* 52 J. Personality & Soc. Psychol. 269, 269–70 (1987).
7. Shelly Chaiken, *Heuristic Versus Systematic Information Processing and the Use of Source Versus Message Cues in Persuasion,* 39 J. Personality & Soc. Psychol. 752, 754–55 (1980).
8. Amos Tversky & Daniel Kahneman, *Judgment under Uncertainty: Heuristics and Biases,* 185 Sci. 1124, 1127 (1974).

A. The Representativeness Heuristic

Most of us are poor judges of probability and proportionality, although we're unwilling to admit it. Rather than perform accurate statistical analyses of probabilities, we tend to opt for the mental shortcut instead because we're unwilling to "do the math." We rely on the **representativeness heuristic** to help us "guesstimate" or subjectively estimate probabilities based on how closely one thing or event seems to be "representative of" or similar to another. In other words, we decide how to classify or categorize information, things, people, and events based on how closely they resemble other similar things or people—even when we lack sufficient information to draw such inferences.

The representativeness heuristic has a tremendous impact on jurors' perceptions of causation. They naturally presume that normal events or outcomes have regular, ordinary causes and that unusual events or outcomes have unusual or exceptional causes. This makes jurors inclined to reject any explanation of causation that seems atypical or extraordinary *to them,* simply because it's not "representative" of their own life experiences.[9] As a result, jurors are likely to question any evidence that runs counter to the way they think things "ought" to happen. Jurors may also assume similarity between unrelated causes and effects or between objects of similar appearance.

One study found that the jury's decision to convict or acquit a criminal defendant may depend on whether the criminal act itself was representative of a particular type of crime. For example, a defendant who abducts a child and demands a ransom is more likely to be convicted than one who abducts an adult but demands no ransom, even though there is strong evidence to support both charges and both acts constitute kidnapping.[10]

1. Perception of Randomness

If we flip a coin to see if it comes up heads or tails, we'll probably do a very poor job of predicting the outcome of the next coin toss because we expect coin tosses to alternate between heads and tails fairly regularly. In reality, however, there may be very long sequences where either one or the other predominates because a true "random" coin toss doesn't *appear* random at all while it's happening.[11] Our perception of randomness is flawed because we tend to focus on a single, small, unrepresentative sample.

---

9. Igor Gavanski & Gary L. Wells, *Counterfactual Processing of Normal and Exceptional Events,* 25 J. Experimental Soc. Psychol. 314, 317–20 (1989).
10. Vicki L. Smith, *Prototypes in the Courtroom: Lay Representations of Legal Concepts,* 61 J. Personality & Soc. Psychol. 857–62 (1991), *cited in* Bernstein, *supra* note 1, at 294.
11. Amos Tversky & Daniel Kahneman, *Belief in the Law of Small Numbers,* 76 Psychol. Bull. 105, 105–07 (1971).

The representativeness heuristic inspires us to believe that past events have a certain predictable effect on future outcomes. This leads gamblers to believe their string of bad luck is bound to end soon. It also leads basketball players who are playing an extraordinary game to believe their "hot streak" will last longer than it actually does.[12] In fact, these are merely examples of random chance at work.

Unfortunately, chance is not self-correcting.[13] This fact keeps casinos in business and compulsive gamblers in debt. The representativeness heuristic biases our thinking and causes us to think that "chance" or the "odds" appear random only in the short run; but it's typically in the long run that randomness becomes truly apparent.

2. Examples of the Representativeness Heuristic

Amos Tversky and Daniel Kahneman did a study in which subjects were told that a taxicab had been involved in a hit and run accident at night.[14] Subjects were also given the following information: (1) There are only two cab companies in town, Green Company and Blue Company, with cabs of corresponding colors; (2) sixty-seven percent of the cabs in town are blue and thirty-three percent are green; (3) an eyewitness has identified the cab as green; (4) the witness's reliability was tested under the same circumstances existing on the night of the accident, and the witness correctly identified each of the two colors only fifty percent of the time.

Subjects were then asked to calculate the probability of whether the cab involved in the accident was green or blue. Most subjects inaccurately calculated the probability that the cab was just as likely to be green as blue. Obviously, they let the eyewitness's claim that the cab was green skew their calculations, which *should have* corresponded to the actual numbers of green and blue cabs since the witness couldn't distinguish green from blue about half the time. All other things being equal, the *actual probability* that the witness was correct is a mere thirty-three percent; but subjects neglected the relevant base-rate information and simply *presumed* the eyewitness was correct rather than bother to calculate the odds. This phenomenon is called **base rate neglect**.[15]

Similar studies have yielded analogous findings. For example, if we presume that seventy-five percent of a town's adult male population is in the

---

12. When the gambler finally wins or the basketball player's performance returns to normal, this is referred to as "**regression to the mean**."
13. Scott Plous, The Psychology of Judgment and Decision Making 119 (1993).
14. Tversky & Kahneman, *supra* note 8, at 1127–28.
15. Amos Tversky & Daniel Kahneman, *Evidential Impact of Base Rates, in* Judgments Under uncertainty: Heuristics and Biases 153, 156 (Daniel Kahneman et al. eds., 1982) [hereinafter *Base Rates*].

accounting business and that a particular man likes math, we're likely to simply presume he's an accountant. But if we're also told that this man loves music, we're more likely to believe he's a musician—despite the overwhelming statistical odds that he's an accountant. Although he's much more likely to be an accountant who loves music than a musician, we'll probably allow this single, comparatively irrelevant factor to cause us to disregard the odds, simply because we don't believe a music lover is "representative" of what we think an accountant should be.[16] If we're told that this man loves music *first*, both representativeness and primacy make us even *more* likely to disregard the fact that seventy-five percent of the adult males in town are accountants.

3. Representativeness at Trial

Jurors use the representativeness heuristic to categorize certain types of people, professions, things, and events. If we can predict what jurors are likely to perceive as "representative" of a particular person, thing, or experience, we can create appropriate reference points in our presentation of evidence.

For example, if the plaintiff was seriously injured in an accident, but there was only minimal damage to her car, jurors may refuse to believe that her injury is really serious because that's not what "usually" happens in such accidents. Jurors typically equate "minimal damage" with "minimal injury" in car wreck cases; therefore, they may presume that the plaintiff could not have suffered serious injury without also incurring significant damage to her car. This presumption will be difficult for plaintiff's counsel to overcome without significant juror education about how many people actually suffer serious injuries, even though there is little or no damage to their vehicles.

Jurors will also compare the litigants to other people they know. This may cause them to believe, for example, that their personal physician is "representative" of the medical profession as a whole. If they like, trust, and respect their own doctor, they may assume the defendant doctor in a medical malpractice case is like their doctor. This may lead jurors to focus on a particular action, fact, or personal characteristic of the defendant doctor that has little, if any, relevance to the issues.

For example, if the defendant physician spent time with the plaintiff and listened to her complaints, this single piece of information may cause jurors to disregard other more important and statistically significant information

---

16.   *Id.* at 156–57. *But see* Jon Krosnick & Howard Schuman, *Attitude, Intensity, Importance, and Certainty and Susceptibility to Response Effects,* 54 J. PERSONALITY & SOC. PSYCHOL. 940, 941–43 (1988) (proposing that this phenomenon is due to information order effects and that if Tversky & Kahneman had reversed the order in which information was presented to subjects, the effects would have been mitigated).

about the physician's actual adherence to the applicable standard of care. Obviously, this may skew the jurors' judgment and lead them to make incorrect assumptions.

We can counteract this tendency by using focus groups and information culled from voir dire to find out what jurors expect from their own doctors. If we know in advance what jurors are likely to view as representative of "proper physician conduct," we can use this information to our client's advantage. If we represent the defendant doctor, we can show how our client behaved *consistently* with what jurors expect of a competent physician. He spent time with the plaintiff, listened to her complaints, and carefully explained his diagnosis and course of treatment in terms she could easily understand.

We can also demonstrate that the plaintiff behaved *inconsistently* with what jurors expect of a good patient. For example, we can show that she failed to take her medication as prescribed, refused to follow her doctor's orders to stay in bed, and didn't return for her follow-up appointment. This simply isn't "representative" of how a patient should behave.

On the other hand, if we represent the plaintiff, we must show that the defendant doctor acted *inconsistently* with jurors' expectations of competence. For example, we could show that the defendant doctor who committed malpractice in another way also prescribed the wrong medication for the plaintiff. Even though the erroneous prescription was harmless, this departure from what jurors expect of doctors will color their views on the issue of whether he deviated from the standard of care at issue in the case. Jurors react this way because prescribing the wrong medication is *not* representative of how a competent, caring professional practices medicine.

Many legal commentators believe O. J. Simpson's acquittal was due to his physical attractiveness and celebrity status. The jurors were primarily young African-American females who did not see the attractive, athletic celebrity as representative of a "murderer"; therefore, it was difficult for them to imagine that he could commit such a heinous crime.[17]

Another interesting example of representativeness relates to eyewitness testimony. Jurors tend to believe and accept detailed eyewitness testimony more readily than less specific testimony because they perceive the detailed account as more representative of how people perceive startling events in real life.[18] Interestingly, the opposite is actually true.[19]

---

17. John C. Brigham & Adina W. Wasserman, *The Impact of Race, Racial Attitude, and Gender to the Criminal Trial of O. J. Simpson,* 29 J. Applied Soc Psychol. 1333–36 (1999).
18. *See generally,* Elizabeth Loftus et al, Eyewitness Testimony: Civil and Criminal (4th ed. 2007).
19. *Id.*

For example, if a man who was robbed in the dark of night can offer a detailed description of the perpetrator's clothing, height, and weight, jurors are likely to believe that his identification is correct—even though he never saw the perpetrator's face and the incident was over in a matter of seconds. The addition of detail makes jurors more inclined to believe the victim's identification is correct, simply because it's representative of how they think most people would respond to a frightening event. Therefore, it comes as no surprise that most of the people freed by DNA evidence through the work of the Innocence Project were convicted primarily on eyewitness testimony.[20]

Trial lawyers fall prey to the representative heuristic as well. For example, we like to think we're good at jury selection because we know what is representative of a "good" juror in a particular type of case. But in truth, random selection of jurors probably yields the same or better results than we routinely achieve on our own.[21]

Similar studies in other professions have shown that "clinical predictions" made by humans, which rely heavily on heuristics, are much less accurate than actuarial predictions.[22] Nevertheless, we continue to justify our reliance on the representativeness heuristic by convincing ourselves that statistics lack a certain human dimension, which makes them inherently unreliable. Unfortunately, this is rarely the case.

B. The Availability Heuristic

The "availability heuristic" holds that we estimate the probability or frequency of an event by the ease with which we can generate similar instances or occurrences in our own minds.[23] In other words, we judge the likelihood of an event or outcome based on how easily it comes to mind.[24] We also tend to base our judgments more on the actual *number* of similar thoughts or experiences we're able to recall or imagine rather the logic, wisdom, or applicability

---

20. For the most up-to-date statistics, visit www.innocence project.org.
21. With regard to scientific jury selection, the evidence (based solely on criminal cases) is mixed. The effectiveness of the process for causing a favorable outcome varies by crime. There is no available data comparing attorney selection to selection with the assistance of jury consultants. For a discussion of this, *see* Richard Seltzer, *Scientific Jury Selection: Does It Work?* J. APPLIED SOC. PSYCHOL. 2417–35 (2006).
22. PLOUS, *supra* note 13, at 18–19.
23. Daniel Kahneman & Amos Tversky, *supra* note 8, at 1124–31.
24. This is technically an example of the **simulation heuristic**, a corollary of the availability heuristic. The simulation heuristic is apparent when people judge the likelihood of an event or outcome based on how easily it comes to mind. Daniel Kahneman & Amos Tversky, *The Simulation Heuristic in* JUDGMENT UNDER UNCERTAINTY: HEURISTICS AND BIASES 201–08 (Daniel Kahneman et al. eds., 1982).

of such thoughts or experiences. This means that heuristic processing may cause us to be more influenced by quantity than quality.[25]

All of us can bring to mind common, ordinary events more easily than uncommon, unusual ones; therefore, we tend to conclude the probability or frequency of commonplace events is high.[26] However, if the occurrence of a particular event is difficult for us to imagine, we tend to conclude that its probability or frequency is low. These tendencies may lead us to confuse what is most easily and readily "available" in memory with what happens most often in real life. Mere ease of imagination skews our judgment as to the likelihood of similar events. The unfortunate implication of this at trial is clear: *jurors tend to confuse ease of recall with frequency of occurrence.*

For example, most of us tend to overestimate our chances of winning the lottery because we've heard so much about winners who have received millions of dollars and so little about the hundreds of millions of people who have won little or nothing.[27] The amount of attention given to big winners by the media leads us to subjectively overestimate their numbers because this information is so readily "available" in memory.

In recent years, the media has also devoted an inordinate amount of attention to so-called "frivolous lawsuits." Negative publicity has made many jurors inherently skeptical of plaintiffs' claims, simply because they've read so much about "undeserving" plaintiffs who have received "outrageous" verdicts, despite the lack of evidence to support such allegations. The memory of the negative publicity is simply more available in juror memory.

The availability heuristic works fairly well when jurors estimate the likelihood of ordinary events in their everyday lives because it simplifies and expedites decision-making. But if jurors perceive what happened to our client as atypical or unlikely, i.e., if the event is cognitively "unavailable" in the minds of our jurors, they may draw conclusions or make gross generalizations about fault that are unfair or inappropriate since what *usually* happens is not the proper legal determinant for any element of negligence.

At trial, our job is to provide jurors with the information they need to reach a just verdict by making it cognitively "available" to them. What we focus on largely determines how the case will be decided.

---

25. This is an example of the **numerosity heuristic**, which is another corollary of the availability heuristic.

26. Robyn M. Dawes et al., *Clinical versus Actuarial Judgment,* 243 SCIENCE 1668–74 (1989). A caveat is in order, however. When jurors are relying on controlled or systematic processing rather than heuristic or automatic processing, they tend to be more easily influenced by the fact that they can only retrieve a *few* similar instances from memory rather than many. They simply have more confidence in their thoughts when only a few examples come to mind. Zakary L. Tormala et al, *Ease of Retrieval Effects in Persuasion: A Self-Validation Analysis,* 28 PERSONALITY & SOC. PSYCHOL. BULL. 1700–12 (2002).

27. BERNSTEIN, *supra* note 1, at 295.

Fortunately, we have the opportunity to control the flow of information in our case. We can increase the availability of important facts by considering the following questions as we prepare for trial. First, how are jurors accustomed to thinking about these facts? Second, how do they *need* to think about these facts to confirm their deeply held beliefs and biases? Third, how much prior exposure have jurors had to similar situations or circumstances? And last, how likely are jurors to perceive what happened to our client as "normal" or "reasonable"? Focus groups and, to a lesser extent, jury questionnaires and voir dire are the best ways to determine the answers to these questions.

1. Frequency of Exposure

Frequency of exposure plays a significant role in the availability of information. All of us have an instinctive fear of the unfamiliar because it's unpredictable and potentially unsafe. For example, we're wary of unfamiliar people, things, and events because they make us uneasy; but the more we're exposed to them, the more comfortable we become. Consider driving a car. It's pretty scary when we first get behind the wheel, but as we get more experience, driving becomes second nature and considerably less worrisome.

The same is true of information. At the beginning of trial, jurors are strangers to the case; but as they learn more about the facts, they grow increasingly comfortable with those facts, particularly if they're presented early and reiterated over the course of the trial. The more "available" certain facts are in juror memory, the more likely jurors are to presume those facts have value.

A recent experiment proves the point. Students in a class were exposed to photographs of several equally attractive subjects involved in the study. The first subject never attended class. The second attended class five times; the third, ten times; and the fourth, twenty times. When members of the class were later shown photographs of the four subjects, students readily identified the most familiar subject as the most attractive. Although the fourth subject was no more attractive than the other three, students instinctively gravitated to the most familiar, cognitively "available" face.[28]

At trial, we can increase the cognitive availability of the critical facts of our case by presenting them early and often. For example, if we represent an injured plaintiff, we should begin voir dire with broad questions to the panel that relate to the defendant's wrongdoing since this is the information we want to make most available in juror memory: What are your views on drinking drivers? What experience have you had with a driver who had been drinking? How about family members or friends?

---

28.   Richard Moreland & Scott Beach, *Exposure Effect in the Classroom: The Development of Affinity Among Students,* 28 J. Experimental Soc. Psychol. 255 (1992).

Availability can also be a detriment in certain instances. For example, if we represent a disfigured or visibly injured plaintiff in a personal injury case, we should try to minimize the amount of time that our client spends in the courtroom. Once jurors grow accustomed to her appearance, they become more comfortable with it. Over time, her appearance becomes so readily available in juror memory that it loses its "shock value." Therefore, to maximize the plaintiff's damages, we should minimize her exposure to the jury since the availability bias may actually reduce the size of the potential verdict.

Similarly, in the Rodney King case, the availability of information affected juror decision-making in a surprising way. Los Angeles police officers were charged with viciously beating King after he resisted arrest for a relatively minor offense. The incident was captured on videotape and shown to jurors at the officers' trial. At first, jurors were horrified by what they saw; but after seeing the video over and over, the officers' conduct began to seem less and less offensive. Because jurors grew comfortable with the misconduct captured on videotape, its impact was minimized. The jury ultimately exonerated the officers.[29]

2. Availability and Counterfactual Thinking

We know that jurors make decisions based not only on their perceptions of the actual facts of the case, but also on **counterfacts**—events that didn't actually occur but which jurors can easily imagine or "simulate" in their minds because these facts are so readily "available" in memory. For example, presume that jurors find our particular version of events difficult to imagine. If they can easily imagine an alternative version of events, simply because it's more available in memory, they're likely to conclude that their imagined version of events is what actually occurred. Alternatively, they may conclude that the underlying event simply didn't happen at all.

Jurors don't question our version of events because it's unbelievable; they question it because they think it more likely that it happened in some other way, a way they can more easily imagine. For example, if the plaintiff is badly injured in a freak accident, jurors may find difficult to simply accept her version of events without question. As they listen to the evidence, they automatically tend to imagine all of the other ways in which the underlying event could have or might have unfolded. If the jurors' imagined "counterfacts" seem more plausible to them than the plaintiff's testimony, they're less likely to believe her testimony.

Social psychological research bears this out. Psychologist Steven Sherman and his colleagues asked people to imagine developing symptoms of a dis-

---

29. Richard J. Waites, Courtroom Psychology and Trial Advocacy 388 (ALM Publishing 2003).

ease that didn't exist (which participants were not told).[30] When participants found symptoms of the fictitious disease easy to imagine, they rated themselves as much more likely to contract it. Sherman concluded that the ease or difficulty with which jurors were able to generate symptoms of the imaginary disease in their minds influenced not only how frequently they believed the disease could occur, but also how dangerous it could be.[31]

We know that jurors tend to indulge in a self-protective form of counterfactual thinking when confronted with a severely injured plaintiff, particularly if they perceive themselves as similar to her. (*See* chapter four.) Rather than consider the prospect of being seriously injured in a similar manner, jurors may simply refuse to fully consider credible evidence because it frightens or upsets them. The very thought of being similarly injured can be so abhorrent to jurors that they deliberately make such information mentally *unavailable* to themselves.

If we represent the plaintiff, we can combat this tendency by increasing the availability of the defendant's wrongful conduct in juror memory. By focusing more on what the defendant did or failed to do rather than on the plaintiff, her conduct, and the harm she suffered, we can make the availability heuristic work for us rather than against us.

3. Availability and Experts

The availability heuristic may lead jurors to oversimplify or ignore complex or confusing evidence and search for an easier, simpler explanation. We know that people tend to be cognitively lazy; therefore, if our evidence is likely to be difficult for jurors to understand, we must simplify it to make it more cognitively "available" to them. This may require the assistance of a competent expert witness who can help jurors understand what happened, why it happened, and why the opposing party is responsible for the bad outcome.

For example, if the plaintiff was injured in a car accident that was caused by a design defect in her car, jurors are unlikely to know enough about engineering and the automotive industry to fully understand what happened. We'll need to hire an automotive expert who can talk about the defective design in simple, understandable language. This makes the science behind the defective design more available to jurors.

Selection of expert witnesses is critical. Often, the most effective expert on an issue is not the one with the best qualifications or the most important job in the field. Instead, the best expert is likely the best teacher of the subject to

---

30. Steven J. Sherman et al., *Imagining Can Heighten or Lower the Perceived Likelihood of Contracting a Disease: The Mediating Effect of Ease of Imagery,* 11 Personality & Soc. Psychol. Bull. 118–27 (1985).
31. *Id.*

laypeople. So, for example, when two cars collide at a low rate of speed, we can call a high school physics teacher as an expert witness. He can use simple analogies like five or six balls hanging from strings that bang into each other to help demonstrate the concept of transmitted force. He may even be a more effective expert than his "learned" counterpart from the big university. Ordinarily, we don't need the expert with the highest level of expertise: we need the expert who can make information most readily available to jurors.

Unfortunately, experts may fall prey to the availability heuristic themselves. Because they know so much about a particular subject, they tend to have preconceived notions about causation based on the availability of their prior experience. This may cause them to leap to conclusions too quickly. If, for example, our expert *presumes* that he knows what happened in our case because his knowledge, experience, and training have taught him to expect that something *usually* happens in a particular way, he may exclude other explanations simply because they're neither "representative" of his expertise nor readily "available" in his memory. Even experts can make mistakes when they inappropriately rely on heuristics.

We can ensure this doesn't happen with our own expert witnesses by meticulously preparing for trial. The first step is to prepare ourselves long before we hire testifying experts. Reading and learning as much as we can about their area of expertise helps, but if this isn't sufficient to prepare our testifying experts, we should consider hiring a consulting expert to help us fully understand what happened and why. Then we're better equipped to prep the experts who will testify at trial.

4. Accessibility and Priming

Closely related to the availability heuristic is a sort of subcategory of availability called **accessibility**. Accessibility is the psychological term that describes how easily information stored in memory is activated.[32] Many thoughts are available in memory if we take time to imagine them, but that doesn't necessarily mean they're easily accessible.

For example, if we say the word "dog" during trial, dog owners on the jury are likely to imagine their own particular breed of dog because it's their most readily available memory of what a dog should look like. But if we ask them to think of the word "dog" in a particular context such as "firefighting," they're likely to **access** a totally different image of "dog" in their minds. Although their own dog's image is usually more accessible in memory, jurors have been socially primed to access a Dalmatian on a red fire truck because

---

32. Colin MacLeod & Lynlee Campbell, *Memory, Accessibility, and Probability Judgments: An Experimental Evaluation of the Availability Heuristic,* 63 J. PERSONALITY & SOC. PSYCH. 890–902 (1992).

it's a uniquely American cultural icon. Therefore, when the word "dog" is coupled with firefighting, the image of a Dalmatian becomes more accessible to them than other, more available images of dogs stored in memory.

To make information both available and accessible for our jurors, we need to learn as much as we can about their backgrounds and life experiences. This gives us insight into how available *and* accessible certain types of information may be in juror memory. We can then use what we've learned to make our evidence more accessible to the jury.

C. The Anchoring Heuristic

Anchoring is essentially using a point of reference when making a decision. All human beings tend to make relative rather than absolute judgments, i.e., we compare one thing to another to evaluate its worth. "As compared to what" is the common expression that sums this up.

Whenever we're asked to estimate the probability of an event or judge the value of a particular item or investment, we tend to reach one conclusion if we do the calculation without reference to an initial value or starting point and quite another if we're given a point of departure or "anchor"—*even if the anchor is completely arbitrary*. Once an anchor is established, we continue to let it affect our judgment by stubbornly refusing to adequately adjust up or down from that initial starting point.[33]

For example, if we ask, "How tall is the tallest California Redwood tree," we will get a much wider range of responses than if we instead ask, "Is the tallest California Redwood taller or shorter than 700 feet?" Once the number 700 has been suggested, it creates an irrevocable bias or anchor.

Anchoring values is a technique that has widespread support in psychological research. People instinctively look for cues to find appropriate answers to novel or unfamiliar problems. For example, if a man is asked whether he considers a certain woman attractive, he's likely to compare the woman he's evaluating to his wife or other women who may be nearby. Although the mind is likely capable of making an absolute judgment without resorting to comparison, he will avoid the absolute judgment and opt for the mental shortcut by using a reference point close at hand.[34]

Studies have repeatedly shown that estimates can be easily manipulated if we provide decision-makers with anchors.[35] Creating reference points or

---

33. Tversky & Kahneman, *supra* note 8, at 1128–29.
34. This is also an example of the **perceptual contrast effect** proposed by Musafer Sherif et al., *Assimilation and Contrast Effects of Anchoring Stimuli on Judgments,* 55 J. Exper. Psychol, 150–55 (1958).
35. Timothy D. Wilson et al., *A New Look at Anchoring Effects: Basic Anchoring and its Antecedents,* 125 J. Exper. Psychol.: Gen. 387–402 (1996).

anchors is a commonly used sales technique. Anchoring is why department stores always seem to have something on sale. The original ticket price provides an anchor for the sale price, which tends to skew our judgment about a particular item's intrinsic worth. Unfortunately, we seldom pay attention to how these anchor values affect our judgments.[36]

Presume, for example, that we're in the market for a new watch. If we're shown a watch of obviously inferior quality first, the higher quality watches we see later tend to look far better in comparison. Our clever sales associate has used the inferior watch as an anchor, knowing it will make the other watches look far better in comparison. This technique is designed to make us more willing to pay for the better, more expensive watch.

Anchors can work in the opposite direction as well. Real estate agents often use anchors to sell homes. If we're interested in buying a new home, our realtor may initially show us several homes that are well above our potential price range before showing us less expensive homes in order to increase the odds of making a sale. The realtor knows that if she "anchors" the price of buying a home with a more expensive home first, the expensive home becomes our standard of price comparison. This, in turn, makes more modestly priced homes seem more affordable than they really are—even if they're actually overpriced. We're still likely to perceive these "target homes" as relative bargains compared to the "anchor homes" that cost far more than we can afford.

Interestingly, we often use anchors that bear no relation to the subject at hand. In a recent study conducted at MIT's Sloan School of Management, MBA students were asked to write down the last two digits of their Social Security numbers immediately before submitting bids on bottles of wine and chocolate without being given any information as to their values. Those whose Social Security numbers ended in higher digits bid 60 to 120 percent more on the items than others because they automatically relied on an arbitrary anchor (the last two digits of their Social Security number) to determine the relative values of the items.[37]

1. "Anchoring" at Trial

The plaintiff in a civil case and the prosecution in a criminal case generally have the advantage of presenting their evidence first. The plaintiff's case-in-chief tends to serve as an anchor for determining causation, liability, and damages in a civil action, while the prosecution's case tends to anchor

---

36. Richard Nisbett & Tom Wilson, *Telling More than We Can Know: Verbal Reports on Mental Processes,* 84 PSYCHOL. REV. 231–59 (1977).
37. Edward Teach, *Avoiding Decision Traps,* CFO MAG., June 1, 2004, at 97, *available at* http://www.cfo.com/printable/article.cfm/3014027?f=options.

the likelihood of the defendant's guilt in a criminal case. This is one of the advantages of having the burden of proof.

It's difficult for defense counsel to counteract the effects of anchoring at trial because jurors are generally unaware of how anchors can affect their judgments and decisions.[38] Once jurors are provided with an anchor, they rarely disregard it; instead, they automatically adjust their opinion up or down from that anchor.

We can create anchors at trial to obtain desired outcomes. Anchors work particularly well when jurors are unfamiliar with the subject matter because they'll be looking for reference points to help them find appropriate answers.

Rules make wonderful anchors. In a medical malpractice case, for example, potential negligence anchors include hospital policies, the medical standard of care for performing certain surgical procedures, and many other potential rules and guidelines. If we represent the injured plaintiff, we can "anchor" the defendant's liability by comparing his wrongful conduct to applicable standards of care or other "rules." (*See* discussion of rules in chapter six, section (IV)(B).) In an auto wreck case, these rules are the "rules of the road."

In almost any context, there are rules that govern conduct. Each choice, decision, or act that breaks one of those rules can serve as a liability anchor. If we use these anchors to compare what the defendant *actually* did with what he *could have* and *should have* done but didn't, jurors will find it easier to blame him for what happened.

When determining damages, jurors instinctively tend to use any salient reference point as an anchor. The plaintiff's initial demand usually becomes the jury's "damages anchor"—the number from which they adjust up or down to calculate damages—unless it's a ridiculous or outrageous amount.[39] Even if jurors believe the suggested damages anchor is absurdly high, it will still put them within our desired "range of reasonableness," particularly if we support it with medical records, photographs, medical bills, a life-care plan, lost wage letters from employers, and day-in-the-life videos.

Defense lawyers are usually reluctant to provide jurors with a "damages anchor" because it provides jurors with a bottom line for awarding *some* amount of damages. Generally, the defendant prefers to pay no damages at all; therefore, providing jurors with an anchor is rarely beneficial for the defense unless liability has already been established and the only issue is how to minimize the amount of damages.

---

38.   Richard E. Nisbett & Timothy DeCamp Wilson, *Telling More than We Can Know: Verbal Reports on Mental Processes,* 84 PSYCHOL. REV. 231, 244 (1997).

39.   Gretchen B. Chapman & Brian H. Bornstein, *The More You Ask For, the More You Get: Anchoring in Personal Injury Verdicts,* 10 APPLIED COGNITIVE PSYCHOL. 519–40 (1996).

2. Anchoring and the Status Quo

All human beings tend to unconsciously resist change. Social psychological studies have shown that most people prefer to maintain the status quo in almost any given situation, even when change would be more advantageous than keeping things the same. We prefer to leave things as they are rather than change them because we later tend to regret action more than inaction.[40] For example, we're likely to keep an expensive insurance policy rather than bother changing to a less expensive policy.

The law has a decided preference for the status quo. We tend to slavishly follow precedent, even when doing so may result in an injustice. Nevertheless, we remain anchored to case law and statutes that may have outlived their usefulness.

Jurors usually view the status quo as an anchor, a tendency that works against the injured plaintiff. To them, the status quo is the injured plaintiff as they now see her in court. For example, if our client lost the use of her right arm, jurors are likely to view her present condition as the status quo. But for the plaintiff herself, the status quo is her life as it was *before* she was injured when she still had two functioning arms. Because jurors are using a different reference point or anchor than our client, it's difficult to convince them to award damages.

After we spend time making the defendant's negligent conduct available to the jury, we must focus on the plaintiff's life as it was *before* she was injured to counteract the jurors' natural inclination to preserve the status quo and render a defense verdict. If we encourage jurors to see her as the happy, healthy woman she was before the defendant left her a person who can no longer dress or feed herself, we have a better chance of convincing them that a verdict for the plaintiff will simply *restore* the status quo rather than *change* it. This is a key premise of David Ball's several books on damages.[41] If jurors see their job as "rebalancing the scales" (restoring the status quo), it becomes easier.

---

40. Thomas Gilovich et al, *Commission, Omission, and Dissonance Reduction: Coping with Regret in the "Monty Hall" Problem*, 21 PERSONALITY & SOC. PSYCHOL. BULL., 182–90 (1995); Thomas. Gilovich & Victoria H. Medvec, *The Experience of Regret: What, When, and Why*, 102 PSYCHOL REV. 379–95 (1995).

41. *See, e.g.,* DAVID BALL, DAVID BALL ON DAMAGES (3d ed. 2011).

3. Belief Biases as Anchors

Jurors unconsciously tend to use their preexisting beliefs (their "belief biases") as anchors for gauging the conduct of the parties.[42] They selectively listen to the evidence in search of facts that support and justify their preexisting beliefs (the confirmation bias). This strong tendency causes them to give disproportionate weight to facts that support those beliefs and may even lead them to unconsciously alter the evidence rather than change their *personal* status quo (their belief biases).

Juror belief biases often serve as invisible anchors in the courtroom. (These belief biases are discussed in chapters seven and eight.) Collectively, these belief biases predispose jurors to identify with defendants more readily than plaintiffs.

For example, jurors have a strong need for protection. They also believe in the notion of a just world because it makes them feel safe. Therefore, jurors need to believe that the current level of safety in the world—the "safety status quo"—is perfectly adequate. They don't want to imagine that they live in an unsafe world because it's too frightening a thought to consider.

Nevertheless, the "safety status quo" wasn't adequate protection for the injured plaintiff. She needed more than the current level of protection, but she wasn't afforded it. Consequently, as plaintiff's counsel, we're often tempted to ask jurors to *change* the status quo in order to make their world a safer place. We want them to feel they'll be afforded the level of protection that the plaintiff was denied.

This argument, however appealing it may be, may not resonate with jurors. In other words, "making the world safer" isn't necessarily a good anchor for the plaintiff. If jurors believe they're safe right now, why would they want to change that? Besides, change is frightening because it presents new and unpredictable threats to their safety.

The better argument is that the defendant wants to *lower current levels* of safety; therefore, a verdict for the defendant would make the jurors' now-safe world a less safe place. It would encourage the defendant and others like him to continue to engage in ever riskier behavior. This, in turn, would cause jurors to lose the current level of safety and protection they already have. (This also taps into the jurors' innate aversion to loss.) But if we focus on what the plaintiff has already lost and what jurors could potentially lose in the future if they render a verdict for the defendant, we have a more compelling argument. Jurors will award damages to prevent personal loss because they value losses more highly than potential gains.

---

42. Greg Cusimano and David Wenner have written and lectured extensively on this subject; indeed, they were legal pioneers in this area. Their "Overcoming Juror Bias" seminars have been some of the most popular seminars ever offered by the American Association for Justice (AAJ).

III. Vividness and Saliency

Vividness and saliency have a powerful effect on heuristic processing as well as perception and memory. The more vivid or salient an event, the more likely we are to overestimate or miscalculate its probability.

A. Vividness

Vividness deals with how vibrant an image or memory is. Dramatic, emotional, recent, or well-publicized events are more available and accessible in memory because they're so easy to recall. A particularly vivid event may seem more representative of other events than it actually is.[43] For example, bizarre or dramatic catastrophes can make us selectively fearful of things that are highly improbable.[44] Interestingly, we remain strangely unwilling to consider the more probable risks of everyday life.

For example, after September 11, 2001, the image of the World Trade Center's twin towers collapsing was vividly emblazoned in our national memory. It caused many of us to be afraid of flying because we feared that we, too, could be victims of another terrorist attack, even though the actual probability of this happening was infinitesimal.

Years after September 11, an Air Force One jet flew over the Statue of Liberty at a low altitude closely followed by a fighter jet. Even though the two aircraft were merely "posing" for a government photograph, New Yorkers who saw the jets were terrified. Many ran out of tall buildings and fled into the streets, fearing another terrorist attack was imminent.[45]

Another example of vividness is that most people believe the murder rate is substantially higher than the rate of suicides in this country. In fact, the number of suicides is roughly double the murder rate.[46] Because of the "if it bleeds it leads" philosophy of local media outlets, murders receive more

---

43. PLOUS, *supra* note 13, at 125–26.
44. DANIEL GARDNER, THE SCIENCE OF FEAR: WHY WE FEAR THE THINGS WE SHOULDN'T, AND PUT OURSELVES IN GREATER DANGER (2008). Although we are capable of reason, says Gardner, we often rely instead on intuitive snap judgments. We also assume instinctively, but incorrectly, that "[i]f examples of something can be recalled easily, that thing must be common." And what is more memorable than headlines and news programs blaring horrible crimes and diseases, plane crashes and terrorist attacks? In fact, such events are rare, but their media omnipresence activates a gut-level fear response that is out of proportion to the likelihood of our going through such an event. It doesn't help that scientific data and statistics are often misunderstood and misused and that our risk assessment is influenced less by the facts than by how others respond.
45. Arthur G. Sulzburger & Matthew L. Wald, *Jet Flyover Frightens New Yorkers,* N.Y. TIMES, April 28, 2009, at A18, *available at* http://www.nytimes.com/2009/04/28/nyregion/28plane.html.
46. *Deaths: Preliminary Data for 2007,* 58 NAT'L VITAL STATISTICS REPORTS 1 (Aug. 19, 2009).

attention in the news. Because we hear and see so much about murders, it's easier for us to imagine that the deceased was a murder victim rather than someone who took his own life.

We can use vividness to our advantage at trial by encouraging our witnesses to incorporate vivid details into their testimony. Because vivid information is more "available" in memory, jurors will be able to better remember what our witnesses have said.

As discussed earlier with eyewitness identification, jurors also tend to predictably, but incorrectly, assume that a vivid account of what happened is more likely to be more accurate than a more nondescript or general account; however, the amount of detail is often inversely proportional to the degree of accuracy.[47] The very richness of our imagination makes us think that we record reality in the same vivid detail; however, this isn't the case.[48] Our memory of an event is much more general and nebulous than the event itself, and the same is true for our witnesses.

For example, if a witness in a criminal case simply testifies that "the defendant robbed the store," jurors are likely to find this account less plausible than if the witness had testified that "the defendant stole a Diet Pepsi and a pack of Milk Duds."[49] In actuality, the witness who focuses on the soda and candy was probably not focused on the perpetrator's face and may be mistaken about the perpetrator's identity. Despite that, a vivid account is more persuasive to jurors because the added detail leads them to believe the witness has greater insight than he really does.[50]

B. Saliency

A closely related concept is **saliency**. An object, person, or event is salient or prominent when it stands out relative to its surroundings.[51] At trial, our evidence may be less than vivid when standing alone, but more noteworthy or salient when compared to other evidence.

Saliency is often linked to causation. If one particular act or omission stands out relative to other potential causes of harm, jurors are more likely

---

47. LOFTUS, *supra* note 18, at 39.
48. Tversky & Kahneman, *supra* note 8, at 1127–28.
49. Brad E. Bell & Elizabeth F. Loftus, *Trivial Persuasion in the Courtroom: The Power of (a Few) Minor Details,* 56 J. PERSONALITY & SOC. PSYCHOL. 669 (1989).
50. *Id.*
51. Amos Tversky, *Features of Similarity,* 84 PSYCHOL. REV. 327–52 (1977).

to connect it to the underlying harm.[52] The events of 9/11 are an example of both vividness and saliency. This horrible act of terrorism was obviously vivid; but it was also salient because the risks of flying suddenly seemed more dangerous as compared to other modes of transportation. In actuality, however, flying is safer than driving a car because mile for mile, we're thirty-seven times more likely to die in a car than on a commercial flight.[53] Our tendency to overestimate the causal role of salient information skews our ability to calculate realistic odds by causing us to disregard all other reasonable probabilities.[54]

We can create salience with exhibits, for example, by making an important fact, thing, person, or event stand out relative to other portions of the exhibit. This encourages jurors to pay attention to particularly crucial evidence. Take the example of two versions of a photograph that shows the injured plaintiff's scar: one version where nothing is highlighted, and another where the area around the scar is circled and left untouched, but the area just outside the scar is reduced in color and contrast to give it a faded appearance. The second version is an accurate depiction of the only relevant thing in the photo (the scar), but the fading creates salience, much like using "callouts" with documents to highlight important language.

In the final chapter that follows, we will see how Mark Mandell, a superb plaintiff's lawyer from Providence, Rhode Island, vividly describes the facts of the case in his opening statement in a dram shop case. This opening, along with a closing argument in a breast cancer case, demonstrates how we can successfully weave together all of the psychological principles discussed in the preceding chapters.

---

52. Shelley E. Taylor & Susan T. Fiske, *Point of View and Perception of Causality,* 32 J. PERSONALITY & SOC. PSYCHOL. 439–45 (1975). In their study, Taylor and Fiske asked six observers to watch two men have a conversation from three different vantage points. Observers who were facing a particular participant rated him as the one who set the tone for the conversation while sideline observers rated each as equally influential. Point of view and visual availability may be the cause.
53. Michael Sivak et al., *Nonstop Flying Is Safer than Driving,* 11 RISK ANALYSIS 145, 148 (1991).
54. Taylor & Fiske, *supra* note 52.

CHAPTER NINE

IMPLEMENTING WHAT WE'VE LEARNED

Both of the examples that follow come from plaintiff's attorney Mark Mandell of Providence, Rhode Island. Because the psychological concepts we've discussed tend to disadvantage the plaintiff more than the defense, plaintiff's counsel is likely to encounter greater juror resistance to persuasion. Mandell does a magnificent job of showing us how to rise to the challenge.

The first example is an opening statement in a dram shop case. The plaintiff was severely injured while crossing the street in a marked crosswalk. He was struck by a drunk driver who had been served a large amount of alcohol at Chen's Family Restaurant immediately before the accident. The italicized annotations point out the major psychological concepts that Mandell addresses.

I. Opening Statement for the Plaintiff in a Dram Shop Case

Ladies and gentlemen, come back with me to May 3, 2010. It is a Friday, and it's early in the afternoon. A car pulls into a parking lot, and the driver gets out and goes to the back door of Chen's Village Restaurant. He goes inside and sits at the bar.

The bartender, Jack Chen, who is also an owner of the restaurant, takes this customer's order for a drink known as a Suffering Bastard. Bartender Jack Chen mixes one to one and a half ounces of white rum, one to one and a half ounces of dark rum, one half ounce of 151 proof rum, and serves this drink to the customer. Shortly after, Bartender Jack Chen serves this same customer a twelve-ounce Budweiser beer.

About forty-five minutes after the customer first arrives, having consumed the Suffering Bastard and the Bud, but no food, he walks out the door to the parking lot and drives away. He purchases more alcohol and heads home, where, during the afternoon, he consumes another four to five beers and almost two ounces of Southern Comfort bourbon.

*Notice that Mandell immediately introduces us to the defendants, which takes advantage of the **primacy effect**. The facts are unembellished. Few adjectives or adverbs are used in his simple but strong sentence structure, which predominately consists of nouns and verbs. His use of **present tense** heightens the emotional impact of what he says, enhances juror memory, and adds immediacy by drawing jurors into the story, making it harder for them to distance themselves from defendants' wrongdoing.*

*Mandell doesn't use proper names for anyone except the target defendant Jack Chen because he wants jurors to focus on him and his restaurant. He uses labels like "customer" and "bartender" because he realizes that jurors must absorb a lot of information quickly. He doesn't want them to experience information overload (**cognitive busyness**), so he keeps the facts very simple and eschews names, which might only confuse the jurors.*

Later this same evening, the customer returns to Chen's, pulls his car into the parking lot, walks in the back door of the restaurant, and sits down once again at the bar. It is about 6:26 p.m. At the customer's request, Bartender Jack Chen serves the customer what is called a Fog Cutter. It's about an ounce to an ounce and a half of rum, an ounce of gin, and a splash, or about half an ounce, of brandy—so the drink contains somewhere between two and a half to three ounces of alcohol.

Fourteen minutes later, Bartender Chen serves the customer another twelve-ounce Budweiser beer. The customer is at the bar on this second visit of the day a total of thirty-two minutes. During this time, Bartender Jack Chen is face to face with the customer several times and for several minutes. At approximately 6:58 p.m. the customer gets up from his bar stool, walks out the door, and gets into his car. It's still light out. The skies are clear. It has not been raining, and the roads are dry.

The customer starts his car and exits the rear parking lot by taking a left onto John Street. He pulls his vehicle behind another car that is already stopped for the red light at the intersection of Granite Street. A third vehicle pulls up behind the customer's car.

*The **addition of detail** makes the story more **vivid** and credible and confirms jurors' **normative belief** that details make a story seem more likely true (**confirmation bias**)—even though studies have shown the opposite is actually true.*

At the same time, a pedestrian is walking down the sidewalk along John Street. The three cars, with Chen's customer in the center, are to his right on the other side of the street. As the pedestrian approaches Granite Street, the light that has stopped the three cars turns green. The first car, the one in front of Chen's customer, proceeds to drive straight through the intersection. After the pedestrian sees the first car going straight, he begins to cross Granite Street in the crosswalk. Just after the first car clears the intersection, Chen's customer follows. He enters the intersection and accelerates as he makes a left turn. By this time, the pedestrian has made it far enough across the street that Chen's customer hits him in the crosswalk.

The driver of the third car, who was behind Chen's customer at the stoplight, is Kelly Vocatura. She will tell you what she sees this evening—but she watches as Chen's customer accelerates through the intersection, into the crosswalk, and hits the pedestrian. She is surprised that Chen's customer keeps driving towards the man walking in the crosswalk. Just before the impact she screams, "Oh my God, he's going to get hit!" And that's exactly what happens.

After the impact, Chen's customer pulls his car up onto the side of the road and onto the sidewalk. The pedestrian, Daniel Earnst, is lying in the crosswalk. Within minutes the police arrive. Officer Dan Turano of the Westerly Police Department is the responding officer. He will tell you that when he arrives at the scene, he notices that Chen's customer has bloodshot watery eyes, has a flushed red face, and has the odor of alcohol coming from his breath. Officer Turano performs a field sobriety test at the scene and determines there are other signs of visible intoxication. He arrests Chen's customer and takes him to the police station, where two Breathalyzer tests are performed. Both Breathalyzer tests confirm that Chen's customer has a blood alcohol level of .166—over one and a half times the legal limit.

By focusing on the defendants' wrongful actions first, Mandell minimizes the **hindsight bias** *and* **defensive attribution**. *He understands that the jurors'* **belief in a just world**, *the* **illusion of control**, *and the* **need for protection** *make them feel compelled to explain why the plaintiff was injured. This often causes jurors to blame the plaintiff for what happened so they can mentally "flee" from the thought of being similarly injured. Hindsight makes jurors believe the plaintiff should have foreseen the outcome that now seems so obvious to them and taken action to avoid it.*

Jurors need to reconcile the plaintiff's injury with their beliefs and biases to alleviate their **cognitive dissonance**. *The easiest way for them to do that is to* *blame the injured party. Mandell makes blaming the plaintiff more difficult, however, because the only facts he makes **available** to jurors are facts about the defendants (**availability heuristic**). This leaves jurors with few options for relieving their dissonance except to blame the defendants, particularly Jack Chen. Mandell also makes the target defendant's actions more **salient** and blameworthy with his repeated references to Chen's Restaurant and Jack Chen.*

> Chen's customer ultimately pleads to the charges of driving while intoxicated with serious injury, resulting in a ten-year suspended sentence, ten years probation, a fine, and other things. When Chen's customer hit the pedestrian in the crosswalk, Dan Ernst, the pedestrian, became paralyzed for life. That's why he came to me and asked me to represent him.

*The **normative bias** makes it easier for jurors to blame the drunk driver than Chen's Restaurant since a common normative belief is that "drunk drivers are dangerous." They don't have similar normative beliefs about servers of alcohol. Blaming the drunk driver for what happened is easy because it's more **representative** of the jurors' own life experiences (**representativeness heuristic**). The American **culture code** for "alcohol" is danger and violence.[1] Mandell capitalizes on this belief by **linking** the target's actions to the drunk driver by constantly referring to him as "Chen's customer."*

*Notice that Mandell doesn't mention his client until after he has unequivocally blamed defendants for what happened. Even then, his client initially remains an abstraction ("the pedestrian") so jurors will remain focused on defendants rather than his client. Mandell knows that the plaintiff was the **last actor** in chain of events leading to his injury; therefore, the plaintiff is the person jurors are most likely to blame when they engage in **counterfactual thinking** and try to "undo" his bad outcome by imagining all they ways that their **ideal selves** would have avoided the injury that the plaintiff did not.*

> Because of his injury, we are suing Chen's Village Restaurant, and we're suing Chen's customer. There are three reasons that we're suing the restaurant.

*Offering three reasons helps jurors absorb information by putting it in manageable **chunks** of information. It also takes advantage of the lyrical quality of the **rhetorical triad** while keeping the target defendant's name in the forefront of jurors' minds.*

> The first reason is that when Chen's customer returned to the restaurant that evening, Bartender Chen failed to assess his cus-

---

1. Rapaille defines the American culture code for alcohol as "gun" because we see it as a sort of powerful, extreme "fuel" for violent behavior. CLOTAIRE RAPAILLE, THE CULTURE CODE 151 (2006).

tomer for signs of apparent intoxication, and these signs were present.

You will hear testimony in this case from Professor Dennis Hilliard and Mr. Michael Marcantonio. Professor Hilliard is the nationally respected director of the Rhode Island State Crime Lab at the University of Rhode Island. Mr. Marcantonio is a master trainer who has trained over 41,000 people who serve alcohol in proper, appropriate, safe servicing practices, as part of the TIPS training program. TIPS stands for Training in Intervention Procedures.

*Mandell lets jurors know that he will call expert witnesses to draw conclusions about the defendants' negligence. This is much more effective than drawing conclusions himself because jurors often share the American **cultural bias** against lawyers and the civil justice system. This, in turn, makes them inherently **suspicious** of any conclusions drawn by us. Expert testimony also makes the science of intoxication more **available** and **accessible** to jurors (**availability and accessibility heuristics**).*

Professor Hilliard and Mr. Marcantonio will explain that a server of alcohol has been trained and has an obligation to look for and recognize the signs of visible intoxication before he serves a customer. And when these signs are present, the server and the establishment for which he works are obligated to refuse service, even if the customer has not been served a single drink.

If an establishment or its employee fails to look for the signs of visible intoxication or fails to recognize them in an intoxicated customer, and serves the customer anyway, and that customer leaves, drives, and harms someone, the establishment shares the blame for the conduct and harm.

*Since discussing the law is generally prohibited in opening statement, Mandell formulates a simple, common-sense rule that every juror can understand (a **"Rules of the Road" approach**[2]). Once jurors know what rules to apply to the facts of case, they will begin to search for evidence of how the defendants, particularly Chen's Restaurant and Jack Chen, violated these rules.*

At least four signs of apparent intoxication were readily present in Chen's customer the evening of this event: watery eyes, bloodshot eyes, a red face, and the odor of alcohol. We know

---

2. *See* RICK FREIDMAN & PATRICK MALONE, RULES OF THE ROAD: A PLAINTIFF LAWYER'S GUIDE TO PROVING LIABILITY (2006).

that these signs were present at Chen's, because they were present just minutes later when Officer Turano arrived at the scene.

Professor Hilliard will confirm that it is physically impossible for a blood alcohol level to rise so quickly that this customer could have left the restaurant without these signs only to have them some five to ten minutes later when Officer Turano arrived. The signs were present in Chen's when he was being served and allowed to leave without any intervention.

Chen's customer had other signs of intoxication as well. For example, if a customer comes in and drinks too fast, that's a sign that their judgment has been affected by alcohol. It's another sign of apparent intoxication. Recognizing this is part of a bartender's training, the TIPS training.

Jack Chen, the bartender, served his repeat customer a mixed drink at 6:28 p.m. That's undisputed. We also have it on videotape. You will be able to see Bartender Chen serve a mixed drink to the customer at 6:28 p.m. You will also see that just fourteen minutes later, at 6:42 p.m., Bartender Chen serves him a beer.

Testimony will show that consuming three to three and a half ounces of alcohol in a one drink, followed by another only fourteen minutes later is drinking too fast and a sign of visible intoxication. Watery eyes, bloodshot eyes, a flushed face, the odor of alcohol, and drinking too fast are all signs that Chen's customer demonstrated that night in the restaurant in front of Bartender Chen.

When Officer Turano conducted his sobriety tests on Chen's customer just minutes after he left the restaurant that evening, he found other signs of visible intoxication. These are included in the officer's report, which you will see. You will hear that the customer had difficulty in placing his left index finger to his nose. When attempting to recite his alphabet, the customer stumbled over letters or groups of letters. When he closed his eyes to do one test, he was swaying. Further, after being instructed how to perform the walk and turn test, he failed to perform the turn properly. Another test performed by Officer Turano focuses on the eyes. He asked the customer to follow his finger with just his eyes while he moved his finger to the far left and right of the customer's field of vision. If a person is under the influence of alcohol, his eyes will flutter as he looks to far left and far right. He cannot control these movements of his eyes. You will hear what the results of these tests mean and that some manifestations of the impairments indicated by these tests must have been present at Chen's.

*Combining auditory and visual elements enhances memory by allowing jurors to encode information in two different ways (**dual encoding**). Involving multiple senses of sight, sound, hearing, and touch not only enhances juror perception and memory, it also makes Mandell's trial story more **vivid** and **memorable**.*

We are not saying that Bartender Chen should have conducted the same tests as Officer Turano. But Chen was trained to do his own tests and to observe his customers. You will hear that Bartender Chen did not look in the customer's eyes, and he did not do an assessment to see if the customer was under the influence.

Chen's customer admits that he had a slight buzz on when he got to Chen's at 6:26 p.m. He also admits that he was feeling a little bit more buzzed when he left after consuming additional alcohol at Chen's. Mr. Chen, however, claims he was completely unaware that the customer might have been feeling the influence of alcohol at all.

But consider what has transpired before the customer returns to Chen's for his evening drinks. He gets up at three in the morning, eats a slice of toast, and works from four in the morning until noon. He has no lunch. He comes to Chen's for drinks in the afternoon. He buys more alcohol and consumes it at home. He eats some chips and cheese around 4:00 p.m. and returns to Chen's. When he walks through the door of the restaurant at 6:26 p.m., he has been up for over fifteen hours and has eaten nothing substantial the entire day.

Professor Hilliard will tell you that fatigue increases the affect of alcohol. He will tell you that in the absence of food, alcohol is absorbed much more quickly and has a much more immediate impact on intoxication and impairment. Given these factors and the amount of alcohol consumed, Professor Hilliard will tell you that the customer's blood alcohol level when he returned to Chen's was at least .10.

Professor Hilliard will also tell you that at a blood alcohol level of .10, and certainly as that increases, the overwhelming majority of drinkers will show signs of intoxication. Now, some people can hold their liquor. But there are signs that cannot be masked. Professor Hilliard will tell you that the reason why some signs, like watery eyes, bloodshot eyes, or a flushed face cannot be masked is because of the effect of alcohol on our nervous system. You will hear testimony about two nervous systems in our body. One, called the somatic nervous system, is at work when we consciously control our muscles, to move our arms or to take a step. The other, called the autonomic nervous system, is at work controlling all functions that we take for granted. This system keeps our heart beating, our lungs breathing, and regulates our body temperature. Most of us sweat, and it is beyond our ability to control by merely making a decision not to.

Even a habitual drinker cannot control whether his eyes get watery or bloodshot. He cannot control how flushed his face becomes. These are caused when our autonomic nervous system dilates our blood vessels. That is one of the ways that our nervous system responds to the presence of alcohol in the body. You can't turn that on and off consciously.

We are not saying that Chen's customer was a grossly intoxicated individual, slurring his speech, falling off the stool, and being boisterous. He was a regular drinker. But there are signs he could not control. Professor Hilliard and Mr. Marcantonio will tell you that Mr. Chen should have seen these signs of apparent intoxication when his customer entered the restaurant for the second time that day at 6:26 p.m. and should have refused to serve the customer any alcohol.

The second reason that we are suing Chen's is because they went on serving a customer who was showing these apparent signs of intoxication. This customer's blood alcohol level increased over 60 percent—from a level of .10 to .166—but the corresponding increase in impairment would have been much greater, and any trained bartender knows that or should know that.

Now, many bartenders measure drinks with shot glasses, so they have an exact measure of the amount of alcohol being served. But, as you will see from the video, Bartender Chen was free-pouring. Free-pouring means that you judge the amount of alcohol based on your experience. You will hear that one reason Chen's customer liked to go to Chen's was because the drinks were strong. When a customer drinks these strong drinks as fast as Chen's customer was and has all the signs of visible intoxication, you can't serve them drink after drink.

The third reason we are filing this claim against Chen's is because the restaurant failed to intervene in some way when the customer got up to leave. Despite all of the signs of visible intoxication, the customer was allowed to just go out and drive. In the video you will see Bartender Chen and the customer acknowledging each other as the customer gets up to leave. We believe that things might have been different if Bartender Chen had taken a few minutes to ask the customer some simple questions: "Are you okay to drive? Do you want me to call you a cab? Do you want some coffee? Would you like some food? Can I call somebody to pick you up?"

*Mandell gives jurors three reasons (**rhetorical triad**) for filing suit to tell jurors that he carefully "tested" the case before suing anyone. This demonstrates the plaintiff's claims have merit. It also combats juror **suspicions and cultural biases** about "greedy" injured plaintiffs who file "frivolous" lawsuits in an attempt to blame someone else for their own wrongdoing. Mandell wants jurors to know Dan Ernst is different.*

*Because jurors often resort to **counterfactual thinking** in order to mentally "undo" bad the outcome by imagining all the things that the plaintiff could have and should have done to escape injury. Mandell counteracts this tendency by creating his own **counter-counterfactuals** that help jurors "undo" the conduct of the defendants rather than the plaintiff: "**If only** Bartender Chen had called a cab . . . ." By showing that Chen had better, more readily available **options or choices** he could have and should have made but didn't, Mandell accentuates his blameworthy conduct and makes it seem more purposeful. This addresses two common **normative biases—the need for certainty in decision-making** and **the need for intent**. Showing the defendant consciously made choices helps jurors at least infer intent to act, if not intent to harm.*

Mr. Chen claims that he didn't intervene when the customer left because there was no question in his mind that the customer was fit to drive a car. He was convinced of this because he did not do a careful assessment. However, within one to two minutes after the customer left, Mr. Chen was proven wrong. Within minutes, based on what he observed, Officer Turano determined that Chen's customer was unfit to drive a car.

So we are suing Chen's Village Restaurant because its bartender and owner failed to perform an assessment for signs of visible intoxication, for continuing to serve the customer even when these signs were there, and for failing to intervene when the customer made it clear that he was leaving and going out to his car.

*Briefly summarizing the facts periodically enhances memory and offers occasionally inattentive jurors an opportunity to rejoin the story in progress, i.e., it offers **multiple points of reentry** into Mandell's trial story. This helps jurors pick up the thread of the story again, even though their minds may have wandered.*

For all the reasons we have stated, we are also suing Chen's customer for hitting Mr. Daniel Ernst in the crosswalk. That customer is Timothy Beauregard, whom you see in this courtroom.

*Only now are both the defendant drunk driver and the plaintiff mentioned by name. Mandell explicitly focuses on Chen's liability first since jurors are likely to see it as more attenuated than Beauregard's. Their relevant **normative bias** is that drunk drivers harm people rather than the* bartenders *who serve them.*

Lest you think that we are simply suit happy, you should also know that Chen's restaurant and Mr. Beauregard have both filed claims against each other. These are called cross-claims. Chen's is claiming that if it is found to be at fault, then the customer should bear some of the cost. Chen's customer, Mr. Beauregard, has filed a claim against the restaurant stating that if he is found at fault, then Chen's should share in that payment because Chen's is also at fault.

Mandell needs both defendants to be held responsible, not just the drunk driver. Therefore, he explains that each defendant is blaming the other, which adds credibility to the plaintiff's claim and distinguishes it from other "frivolous lawsuits" that jurors believe are so commonplace. The unspoken message is: "Even the defendants themselves see each other as blameworthy, so our claim must have merit."

Before coming to trial there were several things that we had to determine. The first thing we had to determine is whether Mr. Ernst was in the crosswalk or whether he was jaywalking. There's now no dispute that he was in the crosswalk.

*Being hit in crosswalk violates the notion of a **just world**. Both the plaintiff and jurors need protection from such conduct. Mandell contrasts the plaintiff's **rule-abiding** behavior with the **rule-breaking** behavior of the defendants. This speaks to the important **normative belief** that we should all follow the rules, and when we don't, justice can only be restored by punishing the rule-breakers. The jurors' primal **need for protection** will motivate them to act, not only for the plaintiff's protection, but for their own.*

Another thing that had to be determined was whether or not the lighting in Chen's bar was so low that it would have been difficult to see watery, bloodshot eyes or a flushed face. You will see from the videotape that the lighting in the bar wasn't that low. You will also hear that it's a bartender's responsibility not to have the lighting so low that he can't make a careful assessment.

A third thing that we had to determine was whether Mr. Chen actually had opportunity to see these visible signs of intoxication. You will see in the video that Mr. Beauregard was seated at the bar for thirty-two minutes. Mr. Chen was on the other side of the bar, of course, but close, looking at Mr. Beauregard during that period of time. Mr. Chen does not claim that he did not have enough time to observe his customer, but merely that he did not.

A fourth thing we had to determine was how Mr. Chen might identify the presence of visible signs of intoxication despite the fact that Mr. Beauregard was not staggering or falling-down drunk, or slurring his words. We had to determine whether Mr. Beauregard, as an experienced drinker, might have been able to mask signs of intoxication. And it was through that part of our investigation that we learned about the autonomic nervous system and the signs that cannot be masked. We learned about the TIPS training materials, and we examined the training program used by the restaurant. Chen's training program contains all the relevant materials from the TIPS. You will see the materials, but, in these, bartenders are taught to look at the eyes to see if they're watery and bloodshot and glassy, and to size up customer and to make this kind of evaluation.

*Mandell describes exactly how he will make complex scientific information more **available and accessible** to jurors. He's **priming** them to hear and understand what's to come by providing context for the testimony that will come later.*

Ultimately, we had to answer another difficult question: should Chen's restaurant be responsible for a customer who buys and consumes alcohol elsewhere before coming to the bar? By talking to the experts and by looking at the training materials, we determined that even under these circumstances Bartender Chen is obliged to intervene. Even if Mr. Beauregard had not been at the bar earlier that day, an assessment would have been required; but it would seem more important given that Mr. Chen knew his customer had been there just hours before.

The things that jurors "have to determine" are the weaknesses in Mandell's case, which he wisely confronts toward end of opening. This helps to inoculate jurors against upcoming defense claims by undermining their credibility in advance. This technique is outlined beautifully in David Ball's books on damages.[3]

> Now, allow me to talk briefly about the harm in the case. One of the important things that you have to decide is what it will take to compensate Mr. Dan Ernst for what he has suffered. To do that, I need to tell you briefly about the harm.

> At the time of the accident, Dan was bleeding from his head and, immediately, he could not feel below his chest from the nipple line down. To this day he has virtually no sensation below this point on his body. He was taken to Westerly Hospital, but it was quickly realized that he needed to be in a spinal trauma care unit. He was transported to Rhode Island Hospital, where an MRI revealed the extent of his injury. The doctors told him that surgery could not help him. He received physical therapy and occupational therapy, and because he was in the Coast Guard and Merchant Marine and is a veteran, he was transferred to the V.A. Hospital in West Roxbury. He was there for a month and received additional therapy. Afterwards, Dan was discharged.

> He was divorced, semi-retired, and had been living in Charleston on a twenty-six-foot houseboat that he built with his own hands. Boating and the ocean were a passion in his life.

*The plaintiff's injuries aren't mentioned until the end of opening because jurors have a strong **normative bias** in favor of **maintaining the status quo** because to change it is scary and unpredictable. To jurors, the "status quo" is the injured plaintiff they now see in court. But to Dan Ernst, the status quo is his life as it was before he was injured. Mandell portrays his client as a healthy, happy, self-sufficient person rather than the invalid he has now become for two reasons: first, it encourages jurors to see the status quo as Dan Ernst as he was rather than as he is; and second, it makes his client seem to be the sort of self-sufficient, optimistic person jurors are likely to award damages to. They want to know he will probably use the money to make the best of his bad situation.*

> Due to his injuries, he is unable to return to his houseboat. He moved to a nursing home, where he lived for nine months. Then, he moved to the V.A. home in Bristol, Rhode Island. That is where he lives now. He's been there for about two years and nine months.

> He has no feeling below the chest. He's unable to walk. He is weak in his upper extremities. His fingers get clenched, but he

---

3. DAVID BALL, DAVID BALL ON DAMAGES (3d ed. 2011).

has worked very hard. He can now brush his hair and brush his teeth. He can almost pull his shirt off. He can actually raise his right leg just a bit from a seated position. He can wiggle his toes a little, but he has no bladder control.

When he goes to bed, he has to wear diapers. He cannot turn himself in bed, so staff comes in, periodically, to turn him. At 1:00 to 2:00 a.m. every night, they put a catheter up his penis and into his bladder to drain the residual urine. Otherwise, he'll get a bladder or kidney infection. He can't control his bowel movements. He has to have suppositories put into him so that he can have a bowel movement every other day into his diaper. He has to have his diapers changed.

He has painful muscle spasms. His hands clench up and so he has medication to help him with that. He can't dress himself. He doesn't have enough balance to stand in a shower. He has to be strapped into a lift and placed onto a chair in the shower. Then other people bathe him, every part of his body. He has no privacy.

He cannot transfer himself from his bed to the wheelchair or back from the chair to the bed. He lives in two positions: in a wheel chair twelve hours a day and lying in bed twelve hours a day. He's lost his independence. He's totally dependent on others for round the clock care.

*Mandell's description of his client's injuries is couched in **absolute factual terms**, devoid of any embellishment or "lawyer conclusions." It is an accurate, **vivid**, and upsetting description that will remain in juror memory. Mandell knows how much jurors cherish their health; indeed, the American **culture code** for health and wellness is "movement,"[4] which plaintiff no longer has. He also knows that jurors can now get a sense of what his client lost by going from a happy, healthy person to someone who is totally dependent on others for care. This taps into their innate **aversion to loss norm**.*

You'll hear about the cost to take care of Mr. Ernst. Medical treatment alone to this point has cost about $250,000. As to his future care—he is only sixty-six years old—you'll hear from three or four people. You'll hear about other equipment that he needs. You'll hear from Dr. Norman Gordon, Chief of Neurology at the Miriam Hospital, who has examined Dan. He will tell you that Dan's condition is permanent. He will speak about the medical care that Dan will need in the future. You'll hear

---

4. RAPAILLE, *supra* note 1, at 80.

from a rehabilitation consultant named Phillip Bussey, PhD, from Bethesda, Maryland. Dr. Bussey has compiled a detailed life-care plan that outlines what Dan will need to take care of himself for the rest of his life.

And you will hear from Professor Arthur Wright, an economist who was, at one time, the chair at UCONN in Storrs. As an economist, he has taken the medical and life-care plans developed by Dr. Norman and Dr. Bussey and has calculated what at a minimum it will cost to take care of Dan. He will tell you that just the out-of-pocket costs for care, including the smallest amount of physical therapy, will be $4,086,000-and-change.

*This amount is Mandell's **damages anchor**. Jurors use the **anchoring heuristic** to adjust up or down from a particular starting point. Mandell wants that starting point to be four million dollars. Once again, he relies on expert testimony to avoid injecting his own opinions and conclusions into opening, which would be suspect to jurors. But he also makes them appreciate what his client has lost, which encourages them to make the world "just" once again by helping Dan Ernst reclaim his **status quo**.*

Dan himself will talk with you in terms of the pain and loss of quality of his life, the past and the future. You'll hear from some other witnesses from the stand who will discuss how Dan might be compensated above the costs of his care. I won't talk about that. You don't need to hear about that from me. You can determine that for yourself.

I would, however, like to leave you with one last thought, because this is important to me. Dan Ernst isn't here looking for any sympathy from you all. He's had all the sympathy one would ever want for a lifetime. He's here asking you for 100 percent justice. Not 99 percent; not 98 percent justice; 100 percent justice. No more. Certainly no less.

*Mandell's powerful ending takes advantage of the **recency effect**. He knows that jurors are most likely to recall what he says last because this information was most recently **encoded** into their **short-term memory**. Again, he appeals to the jurors' notion of a **just world** and urges them to restore justice—to give back to the plaintiff what the defendants took from him by punishing them for their bad acts. He isn't asking for sympathy because appeals to sympathy don't work. His powerful ending **empowers** the jury by leaving them with the ultimate **choice**: they will decide what "justice" will be for his client and no one else.*

II. Closing Argument for the Plaintiff in a Breast Cancer Case

Again, attorney Mark Mandell deftly incorporates the psychological concepts discussed in this book into a wonderful closing argument for the plaintiff in a failure to diagnose breast cancer case. Notice how he unequivocally blames defendant physician whose negligence was extreme.

*Mandell's beginning is deliberately forceful. He knows that jurors don't want to hold a "good" doctor responsible, particularly if there is no intentional wrongdoing. He understands the powerful **normative biases**, **the need for certainty and the need for intent**.*

*Mandell also knows jurors will unconsciously try to distance themselves from the plaintiff and her injury by engaging in **counterfactual thinking**. They will imagine all of the ways that they would have controlled the situation and avoided the harm that his client failed to avoid. Unfortunately, jurors imagine how their **ideal selves** rather than their **actual selves** would have acted. This is how they unconsciously satisfy their primal **need for protection** and the **illusion of control**.*

*Although the American **culture code** for physicians is "hero,"[5] Mandell dispels this notion at the outset. Some jurors may actually believe the strident rhetoric about too many lawsuits causing doctors to leave town. No jurors want to be victimized by "frivolous lawsuits" brought by plaintiffs who want only money and no responsibility.*

> My friends, a simple breast biopsy would have saved Ellen Ward's life. If this defendant had lived up to his responsibility as a physician, as a doctor—if he had recognized the significance of the breast lump that was before his eyes, a lump that he felt with his very hands—he would have ordered a biopsy, and Ellen Ward would be alive today. It's as simple as that.
>
> Ellen Ward died of cancer because on July 1, 2010, this defendant was careless. He was callous. He was arrogantly negligent in violating the first cardinal rule of medicine as it relates to suspicious breast lumps, which is that a suspicious breast lump is cancer unless and until it is proven otherwise. That is the only safe and careful way to save lives.

*Mandell uses the **Rules of the Road approach**[6] and repeatedly states applicable rules of medicine that every doctor should know and follow so they don't harm their patients. He capitalizes on the **primacy effect** with this forceful beginning by unequivocally blaming the defendant for what happened. This counteracts*

---

5. RAPAILLE, *supra* note 1, at 80.
6. FREIDMAN & MALONE, *supra* note 2.

defensive attribution*, which may compel jurors to* **automatically** *attribute* **personal responsibility** *for the bad outcome to the plaintiff.*

Because Mandell knows that personal responsibility is the strongest American **cultural bias***, he immediately casts the defendant as the responsible party, just as he did in his opening statement, to encourage jurors to blame the defendant rather than his client for what happened. He knows that jurors may try to avoid* **cognitive dissonance** *and support their* **belief in a just world** *by simply blaming his client. This sort of* **defensive attribution** *is easier and psychologically more comfortable for jurors than confronting the reality of what happened.*

> Instead, this defendant ignored the significance of a ten-centimeter by two-centimeter lump. That's four inches by two inches, the size of a small lemon. He ignored the significance of a lump that size and didn't order a biopsy, a simple breast biopsy that he could have done himself, or that he could have referred Ellen to a surgeon to have done. He didn't do a biopsy, and he didn't refer her to a surgeon.
>
> And what *did* he do? He ordered two completely worthless, valueless tests. And he didn't even do them that day. He ordered a mammogram, which really only has value if you can't feel a lump, if it's not palpable. Maybe you will find it on the x-ray, but all doctors know that if you can feel a clinically suspicious lump that size, even if the mammogram comes back "normal," it doesn't matter. It doesn't matter because you felt the lump.
>
> He also ordered blood tests. There's nothing a blood test would tell him a week later, or a day later, or two days later that he didn't already know because he felt the lump in his office. He did nothing that day except send Ellen home.

Mandell knows jurors don't want to believe the defendant doctor is at fault because they trust and rely on their own physicians to protect them from similar harm. The **illusion of professional competence** *makes it difficult to persuade them to hold the doctor accountable because jurors experience severe* **cognitive dissonance** *when forced to confront the prospect that their own doctors could make similar mistakes. To maintain their faith in doctors, jurors may unconsciously disregard or alter evidence of defendant's negligence to confirm their* **normative bias** *that doctors can be trusted not to make mistakes.*

> I want to thank you very much. It's been a long trial, and it's been pretty intense. I want to thank you for your courtesy. I want to thank you for your attentiveness on behalf of Ellen and her family.

We're almost at the end of this journey: our mutual effort to find the truth in what happened here; our mutual effort to do justice to the important principle of taking accountability for wrongdoing; and frankly, our mutual effort to do justice, period.

At the beginning of this trial in jury selection and in my opening statement, I committed to you that I would try to present all of the evidence that possibly had any relevance at all to this case. That's why I called so many witnesses. That's why there were so many documents in this case. And now, it's just about time for me to turn that mantle of responsibility over to you all, so that you can carry on the search for doing what is right in this case; so that the loss of Ellen is not in vain; so that the burden on her kids' shoulders and her husband's shoulders can finally be lifted; and so that Ellen can finally rest.

On July first—and that, to me, is the watershed date in this case, and it's where I respectfully suggest your deliberations begin—because on July first, Ellen had cancer.

Mandell invites jurors to begin deliberations at the point most advantageous to plaintiff.

The cancer wasn't small. It wasn't hidden. It wasn't non-palpable so that it could be missed. It was there to be seen, to be detected, to be diagnosed. It was a huge, flashing red light.

The defendant, *this* defendant [pointing], had complete control over what happened in his office on July first. Ellen had gone there specifically to ask him about a breast lump. He had complete control. He chose, he *deliberately* chose not to exercise that control, and he did nothing. It was foreseeable. It was clearly foreseeable that this cancer was not going to be a good citizen and just go away.

*The words "complete control" and "deliberately chose" make the defendant's actions seem almost intentional. This helps satisfy the jurors' **need for certainty in decision-making** by making his bad conduct appear to be the product of a conscious choice. This technique also helps to counteract the **hindsight bias**. Jurors rely on a variety of **self-serving biases** to convince themselves that they could have foreseen and controlled (the **illusion of control**) the outcome, thereby avoiding harm to themselves. Jurors engage in this sort of self-protective **counterfactual thinking** by imagining everything they would have done that the plaintiff failed to do. Mandell dispels these illusions by arguing the defendant was in a better position than the plaintiff to have foreseen and controlled the outcome.*

That cancer was treatable on July first, and it was curable. A simple breast biopsy would have saved Ellen Ward's life. On July first, Ellen trusted this man. She found a lump, and she went to him; and he breached her trust and did nothing. He didn't even tell her she needed a biopsy. All he did was send her home.

Now, it is so basic in medicine that a breast lump is a potential danger that needs to be carefully addressed that even the American Cancer Society tells *us*—not *doctors*—*us,* people with no medical training, that one of the seven signals of cancer is a lump in the breast, a thickening lump in the breast. One of the seven signals of cancer is a breast lump. That is what they tell us. Shouldn't a *doctor* know that? Shouldn't a doctor know what we, as lay people, are taught by the American Cancer Society?

There were two different routes taken in this case. There was Ellen's route: she felt the breast lump, and she went to her doctor for help. Then there was the doctor's route. He felt the breast lump, and yet, he did nothing. And now Ellen is dead. A simple breast biopsy would have saved Ellen Ward's life.

*The last sentence echoes the refrain that Mandell wants jurors to remember and repeat to each other during deliberations. Mandell makes sure that jurors have multiple opportunities to **encode** these words into long-term memory so they can remember and repeat them to each other in the jury room.*

Now, what do you do if you feel a breast lump? What should a doctor do—a careful, caring, non-callous doctor? Well, there are several things you do. If you think it might be a cyst, then what you do is you take a needle and you gently put it in the lump to see if there is any fluid inside; and if there is, it's likely not cancer.

If there's no fluid in a lump *this* size, it's cancer until proven otherwise, and you need to take that needle and take a small bit of tissue out. Just do a biopsy—it's a simple procedure. If this doctor didn't want to do it or didn't think he could do it, he had an obligation to refer Ellen to a surgeon.

That's how you diagnose cancer: aspiration, breast biopsy if there's no fluid, and referral to a surgeon for treatment.

On July first, he never even told her she needed a biopsy. He now says he told her. But take a good look at his records when you go in the jury room. It's nowhere in there, and that's exactly the kind of information doctors put in their records: "Recommended to patient to come back for a biopsy." They put that in their records, and it's clear why he's saying *now* that he did.

What did he do? Or what did he *fail* to do, because he didn't do anything.

Well, clearly on July first, he failed to aspirate what was a palpable lump, or a lump he could feel. He failed to biopsy that lump. He failed to refer Ellen to a surgeon. Therefore, he failed to diagnose her cancer on July first—the cancer that was already there. He failed to treat it on July first. He didn't do a biopsy. He didn't refer her to a surgeon. He failed to schedule a definite follow-up appointment.

Now he says he told her to come back for a biopsy. As I say, it's not in the records. He gave her no definite appointment. According to even him, he said, "Come back in about a week." With a lump this size, you give the patient a specific appointment to a surgeon unless you are doing the biopsy yourself. You give an appointment card out; you make sure there is follow-up.

Mandell highlights each readily available choice that the defendant should have made, but didn't.

I want to ask you this. What follow-up do you think there would have been if Ellen had not paid her bill? Do you think there would have been a letter sent to her with one of those little stickers—yellow, or orange, or green—that says "Overdue"? Do you think there would have been just one letter about an overdue bill? What follow-up do you think there would have been? And what follow-up *should* be done to save a woman's life?

He failed to inform Ellen, as I said, that she needed an aspiration, a biopsy, or an evaluation by a surgeon. He failed to understand the limitations of mammography with a lump. All doctors know that if you have a negative mammogram, but you feel a palpable lump this size, forget the mammogram. In fact, anybody who's seen a mammogram knows that on each one, the first disclaimer is that a negative mammogram is not to be followed if there is clinical evidence of a clinically suspicious lump; and a lump this size is, by definition, "clinically suspicious"—unless you rule it out with an aspiration, which of course he didn't do. So he failed to inform Ellen about the limitations of mammography.

Mandell shows that the defendant again disregarded a medical **rule.** *He highlights other viable options that the defendant chose to ignore. If jurors think the defendant's actions were the product of a conscious* **choice** *rather than mere oversight or accident, they're more likely to hold him accountable because his actions seem almost intentional. Again, this satisfies the jurors'* **need for intent** *and* **need for certainty norms.** *Jurors are more likely to engraft the notion of intent onto simple negligence in cases of extreme negligence like this in order to satisfy their personal needs rather than what the law requires.*

> She called on July eighth, diligently, and she was relieved. No one told her—in fact, *all* they told her—was that her results were normal. She thought she didn't have cancer and had no problem.
>
> He failed to advise Ellen to come into his office when she called on July eighth for the test results. She had every reason in the world to want to live, to be diligent, to be safe, to do follow-up. She felt the lump, and she came to her doctor's office. He told her to get tests, and she went the next day. He told her to call back to find out about the test, but said nothing about a biopsy. And she did what she was told.
>
> She had two beautiful kids, a husband, a good job—she was a fighter. She underwent surgery, radiation, chemotherapy. She did everything her treating doctors told her to do. She wanted to live. And he didn't even tell her the treatment that she really needed. And then he failed to follow up on July eighth *after* her phone call.

Mandell shows the plaintiff did everything she possibly to be responsible and careful to satisfy jurors' expectation that she is a **personally responsible** *person to satisfy their strong American* **cultural biases.** *He then contrasts her responsible conduct with the defendant's irresponsible conduct. He also talks about her loss—two children, a husband, and a job—because he knows jurors instinctively fear potential loss more than potential gain (the* **aversion to loss norm***). Therefore, his appeal is more powerful if he talks about what Ellen Ward and her family lost due to the defendant's negligence.*

> Now, every time any patient goes to see a doctor with a serious, dangerous, or potentially dangerous condition, there is a decision tree that has to be followed. When you have a palpable lump like this, you can either do what's on the left of the chart here, which is what *should* be done. You do an aspiration, and if there's fluid [look on the far left], you simply drain it. Then you have the patient come back in about a month to see if those cysts are still there.

If it's solid, you either do a biopsy yourself and then refer her to a surgeon, if there's no fluid and if it looks cancerous, or you simply refer to a surgeon. Then the surgeon does a lumpectomy or a mastectomy, or other treatment, which would have saved Ellen Ward's life.

Or you could do what this defendant did, which was nothing, which causes the metastasis to spread, which will inevitably happen if you do nothing. You are consigned to die if nothing is done. And then, you *do* die, which is what happened to Ellen.

On July first, this man had two choices: he could have followed what's on the left of this chart, or he could have followed what's on the right. He had complete control of what happened on July first in his office. She was there. He could have done a biopsy, aspiration, or referred her to a surgeon. He chose not to exercise that control and did nothing.

Mandell lists more **rule violations** *and deliberate* **choices** *by the defendant to satisfy the jurors'* **need for certainty in decision-making**.

It was foreseeable that this cancer was not going to be a good citizen and go away. It was curable on July first. A simple breast biopsy would have saved Ellen Ward's life. And now that he's in court, he's saying that this is all Ellen's fault: that somehow what he set in motion by failing to do anything that should have or could have been done—and frankly, anything—any one of those things would have saved her life.

He's blaming her because what was foreseeable to happen, by his doing nothing, came to pass. How dare he come into this courtroom and stand on her grave and tell her children that her death was her own fault?

We all think we have a power to make a difference in our lives: that if we eat healthy or we exercise, and we go to the doctor, we're going to be okay.

Ellen thought she had the power to make a difference. She went to her doctor when she felt a breast lump, and she listened to what he said to do, and she was wrong. She trusted him, but she was wrong to do that.

Well, *you* all have the power to make a difference. You all have the power to make sure this doesn't ever happen again. Not to anybody else. You have the power to send a message to this man: that he cannot do what he did and then come into this courtroom and lie and blame the death of his patient on the dead patient.

*Mandell is empowering jurors to change **status quo**, which they're reluctant to do. To them, the status quo is the deceased plaintiff since they only came to know of her after her death. But to Ellen Ward's family, the status quo is a living, healthy wife and mother.*

Whether we are statisticians, clerks, or nurses, we all have a job to do. And we have to take responsibility when we do it wrong. He has, not to this day, never once—even in this courtroom— been honest and admitted his mistake—his terrible, tragic, callous wrongdoing.

*Mandell again capitalizes on the concept of **personal responsibility**, which usually favors defense, by turning it against the defendant doctor and showing that he never assumed responsibility for his patient, nor did he admit what he did wrong—not then and not now.*

Now, my friends, this is actually, I think, a simple and straightforward case. The issues are simple. Some of the medicine— "metastasis," "angiogenesis"—the words you've heard may sound complex, but the issue itself is simple. A simple breast biopsy would have saved Ellen's life.

Now, to be sure, this defendant did not create the cancer. He didn't do that. But that cancer, as it was on July first, was curable. It was visible, detectable. He felt it. It was curable, as it was created and existed on July first.

What this case is about, is man-made negligence; and in this instance, man-made negligence that caused Ellen Ward to die.

Mandell is now addressing any fatalists on the jury who want to attribute responsibility to fate or an act of God rather than blame the defendant doctor. If no one could have prevented her death, then there's nothing more that jurors must do.

In law school they don't teach us how to talk to juries about money. It's one of the hardest things we do in a case. We can try what we think is a good case, and then we start talking about money, and we get nervous that you will say "That's all Mr. Mandell wanted in the first place. Everything he said to us that maybe we accepted—he's just talking about money."

*Here, Mandell refutes the American **cultural bias** that all plaintiffs [and their lawyers] are greedy and are willing to file frivolous lawsuits in an attempt* *to win the "lawsuit lottery" and transfer blame for their own wrongdoing to someone else.*

Well, I made a commitment to you at the beginning of this case that I would do whatever I could do: put on all the evidence, make all the arguments, try to be as forthright as I could and put everything in front of you. I have an obligation as part of that commitment to talk to you about money. I just do it the best way I can, and I'll tell you how I do it.

Yesterday, I was in my office, and I was sitting back saying to myself, "How am I going to talk to them about money?" And I thought to myself, "What would be, in my mind, a fair value— a range, not one number, but a range of a fair value for this case?" And the number I came up with was two to five million dollars. That's what this case in my mind is worth.

And then I thought, "I'm not going to ask them to do that. I'm going to trust their good judgment, as good, decent human beings, to determine the amount of money that they think is proper."

*Mandell knows that the mere mention of money makes the case sound like a business transaction, so he makes it sound as though he doesn't want to discuss money, but he must. He skillfully uses the **anchoring heuristic** to make two to five million dollars the **anchor** or starting point for determining damages. By suggesting a range rather than specific number, he provides both a floor and a ceiling. Then he empowers jurors to **choose** the proper amount of damages on their own, knowing they have little faith in lawyer arguments. But he also knows that jurors will seize on almost any number that's available and use it as an anchor, whether or not it's relevant or sensible.*

And having told you that, I feel that I have fulfilled my commitment, finally, to put on all the evidence and make all the arguments that I could to present this case as fairly and diligently on behalf of Ellen as I possibly could.

In conclusion, let me just say this last thing to you. Although this case is clear—a simple breast biopsy would have saved Ellen's life—my job really isn't that easy in a way. Sure, I can talk to you about the facts, which are almost all one-sided in this case. I can talk about Ellen's pain. I can talk about medicine. I can talk about the harm it did to Ellen and her family.

The part that isn't that easy is to somehow share with you what really happened here in such a way that you all are willing to see what needs to be done; to care enough to do something about what he did without turning away, because the thought of cancer is so scary, or because Ellen's pain is so great.

The great fear that I have is that somehow you might be scared yourself, as I am at times, about cancer or about Ellen's great pain. Somehow, because of that fear for yourself, you might be afraid of the danger of the disease.

That disease was in Ellen. It is not in this courtroom. I'm asking you to take a step back out of cancer fear, out of the anguish of Ellen's pain, and do what I know—what you know out of the courage of your convictions—has to be done in this case.

*Jurors are terrified of cancer. It's extremely difficult for them to reconcile what happened to Ellen Ward with their **belief in a just world** and their primal **need for protection**, both of which may prove even more powerful than their need to do justice. Mandell confronts jurors' fears head-on by saying out loud that he's scared, too, and that he understands their fear. He cautions them not to let their fear make them afraid to act. This is a powerful strategy for overcoming **defensive attribution**.*

This is a fragile and beautiful system of justice. Justice now lies in your hands as you begin your deliberations. You have the power to make a difference here. Protect our values and preserve this system, because it's one of the few rights that each of us has left. Thank you.

*Mandell now refutes the American **cultural bias** against the civil justice system by assuring them that the system works, despite what they've been told. He exhorts them to trust and believe in the power of the system to protect them and what they believe in. Notice how he speaks in terms of protection and preservation rather than prevention. He understands that "prevention" occurs in the indeterminate future, which is uncertain and often frightening; but the **need for protection** is immediate and is something all of us need.*

*Mandell leaves jurors with the empowering thought that they can protect Ellen's family as well as themselves—and they can do it right now by rendering a verdict in favor of the plaintiff. **Universalizing** their responsibility makes jurors feel they're acting to protect everyone who needs and wants protection from harm, not just the plaintiff.*

III. Conclusion

In the wonderful book *Paris Trout,* author Pete Dexter tells the story of Paris Trout, who was charged with the murder of a fourteen-year-old girl and the attempted murder of Mary McNutt. At trial, Ms. McNutt testifies about what happened. In the excerpt that follows, she is being cross-examined by the defense attorney, Harry Seagraves, about the incident. When he suggests that she provoked his client who then shot her in self-defense, Ms. McNutt replies:

> "No sir . . . I told the truth about it. You can make it look any which way now, but I told how it happened."

> Seagraves said, "That's what we called the jury for, to decide."

> She turned then, looking directly at them [the jurors]. "They don't decide what happened, she said. "It's already done. All they decide is if they gone [sic] do something about it."[7]

Hopefully, this book will help lawyers inspire and motivate jurors to "do something about it."

It has been said that a mind is a terrible thing to waste. For trial lawyers, the thing not to be wasted is an understanding of how the mind works because we can use this information, along with our creativity, to benefit our clients.

---

7.   PETE DEXTER, PARIS TROUT 162 (1988).

Index

C

U

Ultimate attribution error, American trial environment, ch. 7.IV.C.3

Unconscious mind, automatic information processing and, ch. 2.III.A

V

Visual encoding, ch. 3.I.C

Vividness
Dram shop case example, ch. 9.I
Heuristics and, ch. 8.III.A

W

Working memory, ch. 3.I.A

Wrongdoing, rules for showing, overcoming attributional biases and, ch. 6.IV.D